Motive power recognition: 6
BR DEPOTS

Colin J. Marsden

LONDON

IAN ALLAN LTD

First published 1987

ISBN 0 7110 1719 0

© Ian Allan Ltd 1987

Published by Ian Allan Ltd, Shepperton, Surrey; and printed by Ian Allan Printing Ltd at their works at Coombelands in Runnymede, England

Front cover:
Class 56 No 56009 inside the depot at Tinsley on 17 June 1986. *L. A. Nixon*

Previous page:
Displaying a 'Not to be Moved' board, Class 37/0 No 37008 is seen standing slightly proud of the depot building at Thornaby on 18 May 1982. *Colin J. Marsden*

Below:
Two Class 50s Nos 50030 *Repulse* and 50012 *Benbow* stand inside the heavy maintenance factory at Old Oak Common on 26 April 1984. Note that the locomotive on the left is minus its multiple control jumper socket.
Colin J. Marsden

PREFACE

This new addition to the 'Recognition' series deals with all BR depots that have an allocation of motive power. Each depot is given a separate section giving some 'data' at the top including TOPS letters, and numerical location code, with detailed directions of how to find the depot from the nearest publicly served station. In some cases where a town has two stations, directions from both are included. Each section is complemented by one or more illustrations of depot scenes. In the case of larger depots different areas are depicted where possible.

As a general rule depots are likely to contain more locomotives/multiple units during the weekends when traffic flows are at a low ebb. Regrettably due to the constantly changing scene it is impossible to give even a rough estimate to the number of items viewable.

At the back of *Depot Recognition* directions for visits to the BREL establishments are listed.

This product has been written as a guide to BR/BREL installations around the country, directions given are correct to spring 1986, and have been checked with relevant authorities where possible; however, due to road alterations in a number of areas actual walking routes may vary from time to time, but reference to a local map usually found at larger stations or public buildings, should clear up any routeing problems.

In late 1986 when de-regulation of bus services came about some bus route numbers were changed.

It must be stressed that in no way does this book authorise any person to enter railway property, and all visits to depots must be made with prior written permission. Details of how to obtain depot/works permits are given under the heading *Depot visits*.

Photography at most depots is welcome, but as a courtesy, authority should be sought from the official guide in charge of your visit.

Colin J. Marsden
Worcester Park
May 1987

Depots and Stabling Points

Code	Depot name	HST	Loco	DMU	EMU	CS	NPCCS	Sector ownership	Notes	Page
AB	Aberdeen	2	2	—	—	2	—	Provincial/InterCity	—	10
AF	Ashford Chart Leacon	—	2	5*	5*	—	—	Network SouthEast	—	12
AN	Allerton	—	2	2	—	—	—	Provincial	—	13
AY	Ayr	—	2	4	—	—	—	Provincial/Railfreight	1	14
BD	Birkenhead North	—	1	—	5	—	—	Provincial	—	15
BG	Botanic Gardens	1	1	3	—	—	—	Provincial/InterCity	2	16
BH	Barrow Hill	—	2	—	—	—	—	Railfreight	SP	17
BI	Brighton	—	1	—	4	—	—	Network SouthEast	—	18
BL	Blyth	—	2	—	—	—	—	Railfreight	SP	—
BM	Bournemouth	—	2	—	4	2	—	Network SouthEast	—	20
BN	Bounds Green	4	4	—	—	4	4	InterCity	—	21
BQ	Bury	—	—	—	4	—	—	Provincial	—	22
BR	Bristol Bath Road	5	5	2	—	—	—	InterCity/Railfreight	—	23
BS	Bescot	—	3	—	—	—	—	Railfreight	—	25
BW	Barrow	—	1	—	—	—	—	Railfreight	SP	—
BX	Buxton	—	2	2	—	—	—	Provincial/Railfreight	—	27
BY	Bletchley	—	2	4	4	—	—	Network SouthEast	—	29
BZ	St Blazey	—	2	—	—	—	—	Railfreight	—	30
CA	Cambridge	—	2	4	—	3	—	Railfreight	—	31
CC	Clacton	—	—	—	4	—	—	Network SouthEast	—	32
CD	Crewe Diesel	—	4	—	—	—	—	Railfreight	—	33
CE	Crewe Electric	—	4	—	4	—	—	Provincial/Railfreight	3	35
CF	Cardiff Canton	2	4	4	—	4	—	Provincial/Railfreight	—	36
CH	Chester	—	1	2	—	—	—	Provincial	1	38
CK	Corkerhill	—	1	1	1	—	—	Provincial	SP	—
CL	Carlisle Upperby	—	—	—	—	4	4	Provincial	—	—
CP	Crewe Carriage	—	—	—	—	—	1	Railfreight	—	—
CR	Colchester	—	2	—	—	—	—	Railfreight	—	39
CW	Cricklewood	—	1	—	4	—	—	Network SouthEast	4	40
DR	Doncaster	—	2	—	—	—	—	Railfreight	—	41
DY	Derby	2	2	4	—	—	4	Provincial	—	42
EC	Edinburgh Craigentinny	4	—	—	—	4	4	InterCity/Provincial	—	43
ED	Eastfield	—	4	4	—	—	—	InterCity/Provincial	—	44
EH	Eastleigh	—	4	4	2	—	—	Network SouthEast	—	46
EM	East Ham	—	—	—	4	—	—	Network SouthEast	—	48
EN	Euston Downside	—	—	—	—	4	4	InterCity	—	—
EX	Exeter St Davids	—	1	1	—	—	—	Railfreight/Provincial	SP	—
FH	Frodingham	—	2	—	—	—	—	Railfreight	—	49
FR	Fratton	—	1	2	3	—	3	Network SouthEast	—	50
FW	Fort William	—	1	—	—	—	—	Provincial	SP	—
GD	Gateshead	—	4	—	—	—	—	Provincial/Railfreight	—	52
GI	Gillingham	—	—	—	4	—	—	Network SouthEast	—	54
GL	Gloucester	—	2	—	—	—	—	Railfreight	—	55
GM	Grangemouth	—	2	—	—	—	—	Railfreight	—	56
GW	Glasgow Shields	—	4	—	4	—	—	Provincial	—	57
HA	Haymarket	—	4	4	—	—	—	Provincial	—	58
HD	Holyhead	—	1	—	—	—	—	Railfreight	SP	—
HE	Hornsey	—	—	—	4	—	—	Network SouthEast	—	60
HM	Healey Mills	—	2	—	—	—	—	Railfreight	—	62
HO	Holbeck	—	2	—	—	—	—	Railfreight	—	—
HR	Hall Road	—	—	—	3	—	—	Provincial	—	63
HT	Heaton	4	—	4	—	4	4	InterCity/Provincial	—	64
IL	Ilford	—	2	—	5	—	—	Network SouthEast	—	65
IM	Immingham	—	4	—	—	—	—	Railfreight	—	66
IP	Ipswich	—	1	1	—	—	—	Railfreight/Provincial	SP	—
IS	Inverness	—	4	—	—	4	4	Provincial	—	67
KD	Carlisle Kingmoor	—	4	4	—	—	—	Provincial	—	69
KY	Knottingley	—	2	—	5*	—	—	Railfreight	—	71
LA	Laira	4	5†	4	—	4	—	Provincial/InterCity/ Network SouthEast	—	72
LE	Landore	2	2	4	—	—	—	InterCity/Railfreight	—	74
LG	Longsight Electric	—	2	—	4	—	—	Provincial	—	76
LJ	Landudno Junction	—	1	—	—	—	—	Provincial	SP	—
LL	Liverpool Edge Hill	—	—	—	—	4	4	InterCity	—	—
LN	Lincoln	—	1	4	—	—	—	Provincial	—	78
LO	Longsight Diesel	—	2	2	—	—	—	Provincial/Railfreight	—	76
LR	Leicester	—	2	2	—	—	—	Railfreight	—	79

Code	Depot							Sector		Page
MA	Manchester Longsight CS	—	—	—	—	—	1	Railfreight	—	—
ME	Marylebone	—	—	2	—	—	—	Network SouthEast	5	80
MG	Margam	—	2	—	—	—	—	Railfreight	SP	—
ML	Motherwell	—	4	—	—	—	—	Railfreight	—	81
MN	Machynlleth	—	1	—	—	—	—	Provincial	SP	—
MR	March	—	4	—	—	—	—	Railfreight	—	82
MV	Manchester Red Bank	—	—	—	—	—	1	Railfreight	—	—
NC	Norwich Crown Point	—	2	4	—	4	4	Provincial	—	83
NH	Newton Heath	—	1	4	—	—	—	Provincial	—	84
NL	Neville Hill	5	—	5	—	—	4	InterCity/Provincial	—	86
OC	Old Oak Common Loco	—	4	4	—	—	—	InterCity/Provincial/Railfreight Network SouthEast	—	87
OM	Old Oak Common Carriage	—	—	—	—	4	4	Network SouthEast/Railfreight	—	—
ON	Orpington	—	—	—	3	—	—	Network SouthEast	—	—
OO	Old Oak Common IC125	4	—	3	—	—	—	InterCity/Network SouthEast	—	89
PB	Peterborough	—	2	1	—	4	4	Railfreight	—	—
PH	Perth	—	1	—	—	—	—	Railfreight	—	—
PM	St Philips Marsh	4	—	—	—	—	—	InterCity	—	90
PO	Polmadie	—	2	—	—	4	4	Provincial	—	—
PZ	Penzance	2	1	—	—	—	—	InterCity	—	91
RE	Ramsgate	—	—	—	4	—	—	Network SouthEast	—	92
RG	Reading	—	2	4	—	—	—	Network SouthEast	—	93
RL	Ripple Lane	—	2	—	—	—	—	Railfreight	SP	—
RY	Ryde		1	—	5	—	—	Network SouthEast	—	94
SB	Shirebrook	—	2	—	—	—	—	Railfreight	—	96
SE	St Leonards	—	—	2	4	—	—	Network SouthEast	5	97
SF	Stratford TMD	—	4	2	1	—	—	Railfreight/Network SouthEast	—	98
SG	Slade Green	—	5*	5*	5*	—	—	Network SouthEast	—	100
SL	Stewarts Lane	—	4	—	4	—	—	Network SouthEast/InterCity	—	101
SP	Springs Branch	—	2	—	—	—	—	Railfreight	—	103
SR	Stratford Major	—	5	5	—	—	—	—	—	98
SU	Selhurst	—	3	5	5	—	—	Network SouthEast	—	104
SW	Swindon	—	1	—	—	—	—	Railfreight	SP	106
SY	Saltley	—	1	—	—	—	—	Railfreight	—	—
TE	Thornaby	—	4	—	—	—	—	Railfreight	—	107
TI	Tinsley	—	4	—	—	—	—	Railfreight	—	109
TJ	Thornton Junction	—	2	—	—	—	—	Railfreight	—	—
TO	Toton	—	4	—	—	—	—	Railfreight	—	111
TS	Tyseley	—	2	4	—	—	—	Provincial	—	113
VR	Vale of Rheidol	—	4	—	—	4	—	Provincial	—	114
WB	Willesden Wembley	—	—	—	—	4	4	InterCity	—	—
WC	Waterloo & City	—	—	—	5	—	—	Network SouthEast	—	115
WD	Wimbledon East	—	—	—	4	—	—	Network SouthEast	—	116
WN	Willesden	—	4	—	2	—	—	InterCity	—	118
WY	Westbury	—	2	—	—	—	—	Railfreight	SP	—
YK	York	—	1	—	—	—	—	Railfreight	—	120

See page 9 for additional notes on Maintenance Levels.

BR Depots without codes
Cardiff Cathays — Special repair work on unit and carriage & wagon stock
Carlisle Currock — Special repair work on unit and carriage & wagon stock

BR Workshops
ZC	Crewe (Contract)	—	6	—	—	—	—
ZF	Doncaster BRML	—	5	5	—	—	5
ZG	Eastleigh BRML	—	6	6	6	6	6
ZH	Springburn BRML	—	5	5	5	5	5
ZN	Wolverton BRML	—	—	—	5	5	5

Notes
* Level 5 repairs on selected traction only
† Level 5 repairs on Class 50s only
1 DMU repairs due to cease shortly
2 DMU repair level to be reduced to 1 in near future
3 EMU allocation due to move to LG in 1988
4 Depot closes in 1988
5 Depot closes in October 1987
SP Stabling Point

DEPOT VISITS

ALL railway depots, stabling points, yards and workshops, are potentially very dangerous places, and the utmost care should always be taken when visits are made.

It must be made clear that the possession of this book does NOT entitle persons to enter any railway premises without the prior written permission of the relevant authority.

Railway enthusiasts should not turn up at any depot in the hope that a visit can be arranged, as their presence will not be welcome, and could well be dangerous. Any enthusiast found wandering around depots or railway premises where the public are not normally allowed are likely to be removed by the British Transport Police, and charged with trespass.

Organised and properly arranged depot visits are usually welcome at the majority of depots; restrictions are sometimes imposed for operational reasons, and this may include a ban on photography or video work. It is usual that a small charge be made for these depot visits to cover administration, and the provision of a guide.

In the first instance applications should be sent together with a stamped self-addressed envelope to the addresses given below. Only depots/areas listed are presently available for visits.

SOUTHERN REGION
All depots
Regional Mechanical & Electrical Engineer, British Rail, Southern House, Wellesley Grove, Croydon CR9 1DY.

SCOTTISH REGION
All depots
Director of Public Affairs, British Rail, ScotRail House, Port Dundan Road, Glasgow G4 0HG.

WESTERN REGION
Canton
Depot Engineer, British Rail, Canton Traction Maintenance Depot, De Croche Place, Cardiff.

Laira
Depot Engineer, British Rail, Traction Maintenance Depot, Laira, Plymouth, Devon.

Landore
Depot Engineer, British Rail, Traction Maintenance Depot, Neath Road, Landore, Swansea.

Old Oak Common
Area Maintenance Engineer, British Rail, Traction Maintenance Depot, Old Oak Common Lane, Willesden, London.

EASTERN REGION

Botanic Gardens
Area Maintenance Engineer, British Rail, 37 Tanner Row, York YO1 1HT.

Barrow Hill
Area Manager, British Rail, Sheaf House, Leadmill Road, Sheffield S1 2BQ.

Gateshead
Area Maintenance Engineer, British Rail, Traction Maintenance Depot,
    Hudson Street, Gateshead, Tyne & Wear.

Cambridge, March
Area Maintenance Engineer, British Rail, Coldham Lane, Cambridge
    CB1 3EW.

Colchester, Norwich
Area Maintenance Engineer, British Rail, Carrow Road, Norwich.

East Ham, Ilford
Depot Engineer, Ilford Car Sheds, Ley Street, Ilford.

Hornsey
Area Maintenance Engineer, Hornsey Electric Depot, Hampden Road,
    Hornsey, London N8 0HF.

Frodingham, Immingham
Area Maintenance Engineer, British Rail, Traction Maintenance Depot, Dock
    Estate, Queens Road, Immingham, South Humberside.

Lincoln
Area Maintenance Engineer, British Rail, Lincoln Diesel Depot, Great
    Northern Terrace, Lincoln LN5 8HN.

Neville Hill
Depot Engineer, British Rail, Neville Hill RS&MD, Osmondthorpe Lane, Leeds
    LS9 0BQ.

Shirebrook
Area Manager, British Rail, Carlton Road, Worksop, Nottinghamshire S81
    7AG.

Stratford
Area Maintenance Engineer, British Rail, Stratford R&M Depot, Temple Mills
    Lane, Stratford, London, E15.

Thornaby
Area Maintenance Engineer, British Rail, Thornaby T&RSMD, Middlesbrough
    Road, Thornaby, Cleveland.

Tinsley
Area Maintenance Engineer, British Rail, Tinsley Traction Depot, Wood Lane,
    Brinsworth, Rotherham, South Yorkshire.

LONDON MIDLAND REGION

Allerton, Carlisle, Longsight, Newton Heath, Springs Branch
Public Affairs Manager, Rail House, Store Street, Manchester M60 9AJ.

Bescot, Toton
Public Affairs Manager, British Rail, Stanier House, Holliday Street,
    Birmingham B1 1TC.

Cricklewood, Willesden
Public Affairs Officer, British Rail, Euston House, Eversholt Street, London
    NW1 1DF.

HEADING DATA

Each depot has a small technical data section at the beginning, most of this is self-explanatory, but the following will assist readers in understanding the terms and letter codes used.

Location Code: This five-figure identification number is used by the Total Operations Processing System (TOPS) computer, and is not usually used in enthusiast circles. Each station, siding, depot, etc on the railway has a unique identification number.

Gazetteer Ref: This map or grid reference is applicable to the 1985 issue of Sectional Maps of Britain's Railways published by Ian Allan Ltd. The first one or two figures are the page number, the following letter/number are the page grid reference. Note: Not all depots are identified in the Gazetteer.

Type of Depot: This gives the railway abbreviation for the classification of the depot. Each depot falls into one of the classifications below. It must be emphasised that a number of these do the same work and these designations tend to vary region to region:

DTMD   Diesel Traction Maintenance Depot — This classification afforded to Crewe Diesel, Longsight Diesel, is a Midland term to distinguish diesel from electric traction maintenance depots, when at the same location.

EMUD   Electric Multiple Unit Depot — Given to depots that only maintain Electric Multiple Unit stock.

ETMD   Electric Traction Maintenance Depot — This classification is given to LM/ScR Electric depots where similar diesel facilities exist, thus distinguishing the two.

HSTMD   High Speed Train Maintenance Depot — This is a fairly recent addition to depot classifications and covers facilities that deal exclusively with High Speed train stock.

M&EED   Mechanical and Electrical Engineers Depot — This code is given to Slade Green depot on the SR and is indicative that a small BR workshop is present.

SD   Shunter Depot — One of the most numerous types, indicating a depot with a shunter-only allocation. However, main line traction can be maintained.

TMD   Traction Maintenance Depot — This code covers most of the depots, indicating that all types of traction irrelevant of type can be maintained.

T&RSMD   Traction and Rolling Stock Maintenance Depot — This is another of the newer classifications and covers facilities to maintain both traction (locomotive, unit, HST) and conventional hauled stock.

Exam Code: This letter code gives the largest classified exam capable by the depot. Diesel exams are coded A to E (A being of a minor nature, and E being major). Electric locomotive overhauls are classified J, and the word UNIT identifies a depot which caters for multiple unit overhauls (EMU and DMU). From May 1986 revised traction maintenance allocations came into operation, these are shown for each depot on pages 4 and 5, with additional notes below.

Notes: In most cases these are self-explanatory but some terms do need to be explained. The term *Snowploughs*, indicates the number of ploughs allocated to the depot. These are usually only used in adverse weather conditions when deep snowdrifts are encountered and the ploughs are then coupled one at each end of a locomotive.

The letters *BTU* indicate that a breakdown train unit is allocated to the depot. This may consist of a crane with staff/tool/packing vans, or just vans. These are normally only used in cases of mishap.

Some depots are shown as having *a wheel lathe*. This item of equipment is used to reprofile locomotive, unit or vehicle wheel profiles, as correct wheel profiles are essential for safe railway operation.

MAINTENANCE LEVEL

From spring 1986 all open depots and workshops were given a level code, identifying the type of work able to be undertaken. The level codes range from 1 to 6:

1 Fuel Point: Able to supply fuel/water/oil or other daily servicing requirements, manned by unskilled staff.

2 Servicing Point: Capable of undertaking 'A' exam work and occasional 'B' examinations on locomotives, multiple-units and shunting power, this work would also include brake blocking and other work arising. For coaching stock the work could include cleaning, emptying controlled emission toilets, and environmental checks or two daily examinations, weekly examinations or brake blocking. A level 2 depot must have a covered pit, store room and be manned by skilled staff.

3 Maintenance Point: This level of depot will have a Traction and Rolling Stock allocation and be capable of carrying out all levels of examinations and repair work. It must have covered pits, staff accommodation, light lifting tackle and jacking equipment. Multiple-units and Coaching stock overhauls of all levels should be able to be undertaken, plus some patch painting and body repairs.

4 Maintenance and repair point: As for level 3 but having an additional capability for heavy repairs. The depot will be well equipped with cranes and lifting equipment to carry out bogie removal. A level 4 depot may also have a wheel lathe.

5 Heavy Repair Point: A facility capable of undertaking unplanned heavy repairs and collision repairs which may arise at lower level facilities. Facilities should include ability to carry out Component Exchange Maintenance (CEM). A level 5 depot may also have a lower level undertaking at the same site.

6 Workshop: A main workshop with full facilities for undertaking all levels of classified and unclassified repairs.

ABERDEEN FERRYHILL

Location No: 02081
Region: Scottish
Gazetteer Ref: 37 G 4
Original Codes: 29B, 61B
Type of Depot: TMD
Exam Code: E

Classes Allocated: 08
Duties Performed: Local shunting
Notes: Depot also maintains main line motive power. 2×Snowploughs

The depot is on the west side of the Aberdeen-Dundee line 1 mile south of the station, and is visible from the line.

Walking directions: Turn left outside the station into Guild Street, and left into College Street. Continue along South College Street and Esplanade West, carry on under the suspension bridge and turn right into Polmuir Road. Proceed under the railway and a drive leads to the depot from the left-hand side near the park. Walking time 25min.

Below:
A two-road heavy maintenance shed adjoins the running depot at Aberdeen, each track being able to accommodate one locomotive; illuminated inspection pits and working platforms are provided. Class 47/0 No 47109 and Class 27/0 27045 pose inside the maintenance building on 14 November 1984. *Colin J. Marsden*

Below:
ETH Class 47/4 No 47604 stands outside the heavy maintenance building at
Aberdeen awaiting attention to a power unit defect reported on a previous duty,
on 14 November 1984. Much of the building at Ferryhill is of Caledonian Railway
origin. *Colin J. Marsden*

Bottom:
There are locomotive fuelling facilities outside the main depot building; the
immediate area around the fuellers is concreted to provide a sure footing for staff.
Class 47/0 No 47269 is seen receiving fuel whilst sister Class 47/4 No 47525 stands
adjacent. *Colin J. Marsden*

TOPS CODE: AF

ASHFORD (CHART LEACON)

Location No: 89417
Region: Southern
Gazetteer Ref: 6 D 4
Original Codes: 73F
Type of Depot: TMD
Exam Code: E
Classes Allocated: 09

Duties Performed: Local shunting
Notes: Adjacent to the running depot is a BR operated workshop, which carries out a number of classified overhauls to SR unit stock. 2×Snowploughs. BTU

The depot is on the south side of the Tonbridge line 2 miles west of Ashford (Kent) station, and is visible from the line.

Walking directions: Leave Ashford station by the approach road, and cross into Elwick Road, and continue into Godinton Road. Turn left at the end into Chart Road and the depot entrance is on the left just past the railway overbridge. Walking time 30min.

Below:
Adjacent to the running and maintenance depot of AF is Chart Leacon Repair Shop, which undertakes a number of classified and casual overhauls to SR EMU and DMU stock. This 1961 view inside the repair area shows BR 4-EPB Unit No 5320 and 4-CEP No 7140 receiving attention.   *BR*

TOPS CODE: AN

ALLERTON

Location No: 36191
Region: Midland
Gazetteer Ref: 45 E 4
Original Codes: 8J
Type of Depot: TMD
Exam Code: A

Classes Allocated: 08
Duties Performed: Local shunting, Liverpool suburban passenger
Notes: Wheel lathe

The depot is on the north side of the Allerton-Hunts Cross line, east of Allerton station, and is visible from the line.

Walking directions: From Allerton: Turn right outside the station into Woolton Road, turn right again just before the Allerton Arms Hotel, and a private road leads to the depot. Walking time 10min.

From Garston: Turn left outside the station in the approach road, and left again into Woolton Road, passing Allerton station — directions thence as above.

Below:
Allerton depot, situated between Runcorn and Liverpool Lime Street, is responsible for the supply and maintenance of diesel and electric main line and shunting power throughout the Liverpool area. In this February 1983 illustration a line-up of Class 08s can be seen, with No 08923 on the left, and Nos 08018/270/857/887/273/291 on the right.   *David Nicholas*

AYR

Location No: 08614
Region: Scottish
Gazetteer Ref: 29 F 3
Original Codes: 30D, 67C
Type of Depot: TMD
Exam Code: B

Classes Allocated: 08, 101, 105, 107
Duties Performed: Local shunting, and Ayrshire passenger workings
Notes: Depot also maintains main line motive power. 2×Snowploughs

The depot is on the east side of the Glasgow-Ayr line south of Newton-on-Ayr station, and is visible from the line.

Walking directions: From Newton-on-Ayr: Turn right outside the station into Falkland Park Road, and right again along Prestwick Road crossing the railway bridge, fork left into Viewfield Road, and a footbridge leads to the depot from the left side. Walking time 10min.

From Ayr: Turn left outside Ayr station into Station Road, continuing to the first roundabout, turning left into John Street; carry on past the next roundabout into Allison Street, and at the next roundabout turn right into Viewfield Road, and a footbridge leads from the left side to the depot. Walking time 20min.

Below:
The maintenance depot at Ayr is responsible for an allocation of some shunting locomotives and a number of DMU vehicles. Although some of the original Glasgow & South Western buildings still exist, much of the depot has been rebuilt. This view shows a modern part of the depot with Class 08 No 08344, Class 20 No 20099 and a now withdrawn Class 126 DMU. Photograph taken in June 1977.
Brian Morrison

TOPS CODE: BD

BIRKENHEAD NORTH

Location No: 38155
Region: Midland
Gazetteer Ref: 45 F 4
Original Codes: None
Type of Depot: TMD

Exam Code: Unit
Classes Allocated: 03, 97, 508, Departmental 501
Duties Performed: Liverpool suburban passenger

The depot is on the east side of the line north of the station, and is visible from the line.

Walking directions: Turn right outside Birkenhead North station into the approach road. Turn right again into Stanley Road, and the depot entrance is a flight of steps on the left, after crossing the railway. Walking time 5min.

Below:
Until early 1986 Birkenhead boasted two depots — Mollington Street and North, but today only North remains, looking after EMUs and some locomotives; as well as stabling sidings there are also small workshop facilities. Class 507 EMU No 507030 receives attention to its DMS in October 1982.   *G. Darley*

BOTANIC GARDENS

Location No: 19101
Region: Eastern
Gazetteer Ref: 22 D 3
Original Codes: 50C
Type of Depot: TMD
Exam Code: A

Classes Allocated: 101, 108, 111*, CS
Duties Performed: Local shunting and Humberside local passenger

The depot is situated on a spur from the Cottingham line, some ¾ mile east of Hull station, and is visible from the line.

Walking directions: Turn left outside the station into Ferensway and then take the fifth left into Spring Bank, turn left into Derrington Street, and right into Kimberley Street. The depot entrance is at the end of this cul-de-sac. Walking time 25min.

* Depot officially lost its allocation in spring 1987, although at the time of writing some DMU stock was still allocated, scheduled to close in near future.

Below:
Botanic Gardens depot is basically a DMU maintenance facility. Heavy maintenance facilities exist for unit stock, for which the depot was built. A number of main line locomotives are often stabled at the depot. This view taken when Class 03s were still allocated to BG shows a Class 101 inside the maintenance depot, and No 03112 stabled to the side. *Brian Morrison*

BARROW HILL

Location No: 27212
Region: Eastern
Gazetteer Ref: 41 B 3
Original Codes: 41E
Type of Depot: SD
Exam Code: A

Classes Allocated: 08*
Duties Performed: Local shunting
Notes: Depot also maintains main line traction

The depot is on the Chesterfield-Woodhouse line, east of the now closed Barrow Hill station, and is not visible from the line.

Bus directions: Board an East Midland bus No 9, 49 or 59 (Eckington) at Chesterfield station approach road and alight at Barrow Hill station (closed). Walk back 100yd to the crossroads. A drive leads to the depot from the cross-roads. Journey time 25min.

* Depot lost allocation in spring 1987.

Below:
Barrow Hill depot near Chesterfield is one of the few still to retain an active roundhouse, where locomotive stabling roads are fed by a central turntable; some outside stabling sidings are also provided. Although the BH allocation consisted of only four Class 08s, a large number of main line locomotives are stabled at the depot, particularly at weekends. This illustration shows a Class 47/0, two Class 20s and a Class 56 sharing stabling space. *Colin J. Marsden*

BRIGHTON

Location No: 87983
Region: Southern
Gazetteer Ref: 5 F 3
Original Codes: 75A. BTN, BTON
Type of Depot: TMD
Exam Code: A, Unit

Classes Allocated: 421, 422, 423
Duties Performed: SR Central section main/suburban passenger services
Notes: Depot also maintains main line diesel and electro-diesel locomotives. BTU

The depot lies to the north of the station in the fork of the Haywards Heath and Worthing lines and is visible from the line.

Walking directions: Turn right outside the station into Terminus Road (which runs parallel to the railway) and continue into Howard Place. Turn right into New Zealand Road and left into York Grove and at the end turn right again into Old Shoreham Road. The entrance to the depot is on the left. Walking time 10min.

Below:
The main Southern Region Central section express stock base is Brighton, where the depot is located between Preston Park and Brighton stations. The facility consists of a main EMU servicing and repair shop, and a locomotive stabling point. This view taken inside the EMU depot shows one of the now reformed 4-VEG units stabled between duties. *Brian Morrison*

The Brighton allocation of EMUs stood at 183 units, formed of 732 coaches, during early 1986. However, there is insufficient space to accommodate all sets at one time! Two Brighton Class 421 (4-CIG) units Nos 7324/7301 are seen in Nos 4 and 5 roads. Each road in the main covered shed area can accommodate 12 cars.
Brian Morrison

Bottom:
In addition to maintaining EMU stock, Brighton also undertakes stabling and service checks to main line diesel and electro-diesel traction, with members of Classes 33, 47 and 73 being regular visitors. Usually locomotives are stabled in an area towards the station. This view taken on 8 November 1981 shows Class 33/0s Nos 33059/19, and Class 73/1s Nos 73123/138 in the yard.   *Colin J. Marsden*

TOPS CODE: BM

BOURNEMOUTH

Location No: 86923
Region: Southern
Gazetteer Ref: 3 F S
Original Codes: 70F(Sub), 71B(Sub)
Type of Depot: EMUD
Exam Code: Unit

Classes Allocated: 423, 432, 438, 492
Duties Performed: Waterloo-Bournemouth and SWD main line services
Notes: Depot also maintains main line diesel and electro-diesel locomotives

The depot is at the end of a short spur on the south side of the main Weymouth line near Branksome and is not visible from the line.

Walking directions: Turn left outside Branksome station into Poole Road and continue for about ½ mile. At the first roundabout turn left into Wessex Way and then first right into Princess Road. Continue into Prince of Wales Road and turn left into Nelson Road, immediately after the railway overbridge. The depot is on the left-hand side. Walking time 20min.

Below:
Located near the site of the former Bournemouth West station is Bournemouth depot. This is an EMU depot whose prime responsibility is the Waterloo-Weymouth line. Two buildings form the depot, the Carriage Servicing depot — left in illustration, and the Maintenance Factory — right in illustration. Fuel facilities are provided for visiting diesel, or electro-diesel locomotives.   *Keith Grafton*

BOUNDS GREEN

Location No: 54101
Region: Eastern
Original Codes: None
Type of Depot: T & RSMD
Exam Code: A, Unit
Classes Allocated: 254, CS

Duties Performed: Local shunting and ECML passenger diagrams
Notes: Depot also maintains main line diesel locomotives

The depot is on the east side of the line north of Alexandra Palace station.

Walking directions: Turn left outside the main entrance of Alexandra Palace (east side) into Station Road. Turn right at the end of this road into Bridge Road and the depot entrance is on the left. Walking time 5min.

Below:
One of the newer purpose-built traction depots is Bounds Green, which has taken over traction maintenance at the London end of the ECML, replacing facilities at King's Cross and Finsbury Park. The depot consists of a nine-road covered shed, with outside storage sidings. The depot allocation consists of Class 08s, IC125s and Coaching Stock vehicles, although a number of main line locomotives visit the depot each day. No 47660 is seen outside the depot on 24 February 1987.
Colin J. Marsden

BURY

Location No: 31024
Region: Midland
Gazetteer Ref: 45 B 2
Original Codes: None
Type of Depot: EMUD

Exam Code: Unit
Classes Allocated: 504
Duties Performed:
    Manchester-Bury line

The depot is on the west side of the Manchester-Bury line, south of the station and is visible from the Bury-Radcliffe line.

Walking directions: Outside Bury station turn left into Interchange, and left into Knowsley Street, cross Augouleme Way, and continue on to the junction of Manchester Road. Cross this road to the Jolly Waggoner public house, and turn right into Baron Street. The depot entrance will be found on the left. Walking time 10min.

Below:
The only 1,200V dc electric depot on BR is Bury, maintaining the Class 504 2-car Manchester-Bury stock. This depot, which consists of a covered shed and open storage sidings, has to carry out all servicing and repair work to the Class 504s. DTS No 77177 is seen inside the shed on 6 February 1984. *Richard Fox*

BRISTOL BATH ROAD

Location No: 81800
Region: Western
Gazetteer Ref: 3 A 2
Original Codes: 82A
Type of Depot: TMD
Exam Code: E

Classes Allocated: 08, 31, 37, 47, 56, 108, 117, 118
Duties Performed: Shunting, local and main line passenger and freight
Notes: 2×Snowploughs. BTU

The depot is on the east side of the line south of Temple Meads station and is visible from the station.

Walking directions: Leave Temple Meads station by the approach road and turn left at the end into Temple Gate and continue into Bath Road. The depot entrance is on the left just past the railway underbridge. Walking time 10min.

Below:
One of the most important WR depots is Bristol Bath Road, which looks after all Bristol division motive power requirements. The depot is situated adjacent to Bristol Temple Meads station which offers good views of depot operations. In this night study taken from the platform a Class 33/0, 31/4 and 45/1 are seen inside the fuelling shed, while examples of Classes 31 and 47 are stabled nearby.
Colin J. Marsden

Below:
Bath Road is fully equipped to undertake most types of overhaul on Classes 08, 31, 37, 45, 47 and 56 locomotives as well as DMU stock. Standing outside one of the repair sheds is Class 45/0 No 45036, while in the adjacent road part of the depot's breakdown train unit can be seen. BR depot also carries out maintenance work for locomotives operating in the Westbury area. *Colin J. Marsden*

Bottom:
View inside the Inspection shed at Bath Road, showing the deep illuminated inspection pits. Fuel and water supply lines are seen on the walkway between the locomotives. This illustration, taken on 23 December 1981, shows Class 40 No 40141 receiving attention prior to working the 20.25 Bristol-Glasgow parcels, a regular Class 40 duty at that time. *Graham Scott-Lowe*

TOPS CODE: BS

BESCOT

Location No: 65702
Region: Midland
Gazetteer Ref: 13 A 3
Original Codes: 2F
Type of Depot: TMD
Exam Code: C

Classes Allocated: 08, 20, 31, 47
Duties Performed: Local shunting, local and main line passenger and freight
Notes: 2×Snowploughs. BTU

The depot is adjacent to the station on the west side of the line, and is at the north end of Bescot Marshalling yard.

Walking directions: From Bescot station a boarded crossing leads to the depot from the north end of the down platform.

NOTE: Visitors should obtain staff permission before crossing the lines.

Below:
The largest of the West Midland depots is Bescot with an allocation in 1986 of Classes 08, 20, 31 and 47. Two locomotives of special note are Class 08 Nos 08841/832 (illustrated); these are fitted with water skirts for operation through Oxley carriage washing machine. *Michael J. Collins*

Below:
As well as being responsible for its own allocation, BS carries out running/servicing checks to a variety of visiting types. On 23 June 1984 WR Class 56 No 56038 *Western Mail* is seen in the depot yard in company with a Class 25, several Class 08s and the depot's 75-ton breakdown crane.
Michael J. Collins

Bottom:
Quite reasonable views of Bescot depot and locomotive yard can be obtained from the station, where this March 1986 illustration was taken, showing Class 20 No 20019, Class 47/0 No 47299 and Class 25/3 No 25279.   *John Tuffs*

TOPS CODE: BX

BUXTON

Location No: 34202
Region: Midland
Gazetteer Ref: 15 A 4
Original Codes: 9L
Type of Depot: TMD
Exam Code: A, Unit
Classes Allocated: 104, 108

Duties Performed:
Manchester suburban passenger services
Notes: Also maintains main line locomotives involved in Peak District freight operations. 2×Snowploughs. BTU

The depot is at the north end of the station and is visible from the platforms.

Walking directions: A path leads from the side of the station platform to the depot. Walking time 3min.

Below:
Buxton depot, located in the Peak District of Derbyshire, is primarily a DMU depot, but undertakes an amount of main line locomotive maintenance to those machines operating on Peak Forest freight diagrams. A line-up of motive power consisting of Class 20 No 20186, Class 25/3 No 25244 and Class 20 Nos 20141/195 are seen outside the depot on 21 February 1985. *Colin J. Marsden*

Below:
Covered accommodation at Buxton consists of a 2-track shed, provided with side working platforms and inspection pits; between the two roads, under the walkway, service equipment and large tools are stored. Two BX Class 104 sets Nos BX483 and BX491 are seen inside the depot on 21 February 1985.
Colin J. Marsden

Bottom:
Locomotive and DMU fuelling and water facilities are located just outside the shed building and can replenish supplies on two locomotives/vehicles simultaneously. A number of vehicle storage and stabling sidings are provided between the depot and the running lines. Note: some DMU stock is stabled in the station area.
Colin J. Marsden

BLETCHLEY

Location No: 70302
Region: Midland
Gazetteer Ref: 10 D 2
Original Codes: 1E
Type of Depot: TMD
Exam Code: A, unit
Classes Allocated: 08, 104, 108, 122, 310, 312

Duties Performed: Local shunting, suburban DMU passenger, Euston-Birmingham line

Notes: Depot also maintains main line diesel and electric traction as well as unit stock allocated to ME.

The depot is on the north side of the Bletchley-Bedford line just over ¼ mile from the station. The depot is visible from the line.

Walking directions: Turn left outside the station and descend the steps into Buckingham Road. Turn left and continue along Bletchley Road under the railway bridge. Turn left at the junction with the A5 and left into the access road, then left into First Avenue. A drive leads from the left side to the depot. Walking time 25min.

Below:
Bletchley depot has an allocation of Class 08 shunting power, plus the Class 310, 312/2 EMUs and Class 104, 108, 122 DMU stock. In addition, ac electric locomotives are accommodated and main line diesels that operate in the area are maintained. ME-allocated DMU stock also pays regular visits for programmed maintenance. This picture shows the depot yard housing DMU and Class 310 unit stock as well as Classes 25 and 31 locomotives.   *Brian Morrison*

ST BLAZEY

Location No: 85222
Region: Western
Gazetteer Ref: 1 D 3
Original Codes: 83E/84B
Type of Depot: SD
Exam Code: A
Classes Allocated: 08

Duties Performed: Local shunting
Notes: Depot is also responsible for daily maintenance of 'Cornish Railways' freight locomotives

The depot is on the west side of the line between Par and St Blazey station (closed).

Walking directions: Turn right outside Par station along a cinder path running parallel to the railway. At the end turn right under a railway bridge and over a level crossing. Bear right along the A3082 and the depot entrance is on the right-hand side. (The entrance is not obvious.) Walking time 10min.

Below:
The major hub of rail activity in Cornwall is around St Blazey (Par). Most of the area's freight traffic, consisting mainly of china clay, is to be found here, and to provide motive power for these services the former steam depot of St Blazey is retained as a diesel servicing point. Although the depot only has an allocation of two Class 08s, a number of main line locomotives of Classes 37, 47 and 50 are regular visitors. A Class 37/0 and two Class 50s are seen inside the shed building in this night study. This part of the depot closed in May 1987. *Brian Morrison*

TOPS CODE: CA

CAMBRIDGE

Location No: 47215
Region: Eastern
Gazetteer Ref: 11 C3
Original Codes: 31A
Type of Depot: TMD

Exam Code: A
Classes Allocated: 101, 105, 114, 120, CS*
Duties Performed: Local shunting, local passenger
Notes: 2×Snowploughs

The depot is on the east side of the King's Lynn-Cambridge line, north of the station and is visible from the line.

Walking directions: Cross the station entrance into Station Road, and turn right into Tennison Road and first right into Devonshire Street. At the end turn right into Mill Road, cross the railway and turn left into Sedwick Road and continue into Cromwell Road. Turn left at the end into Coldhams Lane, and fork right into Coldhams Road (low level road). The depot entrance is on the left. Walking time 25min.

* Depot officially lost its allocation in spring 1987, but at the time of writing some DMU stock was still allocated.

Below:
The depot at Cambridge, consisting mainly of a 3-road shed with outside storage sidings, is home for the Cambridgeshire DMU fleet as well as a handful of Class 08s deployed in local yards on shunting duties; the depot is also responsible for the maintenance of some coaching stock vehicles. A Class 101 and four Mk 2b vehicles are seen inside the depot building. *Brian Morrison*

TOPS CODE: CC

CLACTON

Location No: 50022
Region: Eastern
Gazetteer Ref: 12 F 3
Original Codes: None
Type of Depot: EMUD

Exam Code: Unit
Classes Allocated: 302, 308, 309, 312, 313
Duties Performed: ER inner/outer suburban passenger

The depot is on the west of the line adjacent to the station, and is visible from the line.

Walking directions: Leave the station by the Platform 4 exit, and turn right into Carnarvon Road. The depot entrance is on the right. Walking time 5min.

Below:
One of the more modern purpose-built EMU servicing depots is Clacton, which currently has an allocation of Classes 302, 308, 309, 312 and 313 EMUs. In common with most of the newer generation facilities, illuminated pits and side platforms are provided to assist staff. Two Class 308 units and a Class 309 coach are seen inside the building in August 1984. *Michael J. Collins*

TOPS CODE: CD

CREWE DIESEL

Location No: 42135
Region: Midland
Gazetteer Ref: 15 C 2
Original Codes: 5A
Type of Depot: DTMD
Exam Code: E
Classes Allocated: 08, 47

Duties Performed: Local shunting, main/local passenger and freight

Notes: This depot also carries out service and maintenance to a number of locomotives from other depots. Wheel lathe. 2×Snowploughs. BTU

The depot is on the west side of the main line south of the station, and is visible from the line, and the south end of the platforms.

Walking directions: Turn left outside the station and first left into a private road leading past the parcels office to the depot. Walking time 5min.

Below:
One of the most important LMR diesel depots is Crewe, which in 1986 held an allocation of 179 locomotives made up of Classes 08 and 47. The depot contains facilities for all kinds of service examination, and also has a wheel lathe, which is visited by a number of locomotives from other depots. Class 25 No 25176 and two Class 47s are seen at the south end of the depot.   *Colin J. Marsden*

Although Crewe has an electric depot some ac electric traction visits CD, this is usually confined to locomotives stabled in the depot yard but occasionally 25kV electrics visit the main depot for tyre turning on the wheel lathe. In this unrepeatable illustration Class 50 No D435 and Class 84 No 84007 in company with a Class 24 pose inside the depot building. *Colin J. Marsden*

Bottom:
The main depot building at CD is of the through type with locomotives able to pass right through on some roads, thus providing outside stabling at both ends of the building. One of CD's additional activities is the recommissioning of main line diesels that have received attention at BREL Crewe. ETH Class 47/4 No 47454 and Class 40 No 40022 stand at the north end of the depot in mid-1979.
Colin J. Marsden

CREWE ELECTRIC

Location No: 42123
Region: Midland
Gazetteer Ref: 15 C 2
Original Codes: 5H
Type of Depot: ETMD
Exam Code: J, Unit
Classes Allocated: 85, 304

Duties Performed: Local and WCML electric passenger/freight

Notes: This depot also maintains a large number of LMR/ScR 25kV electric locomotives

The depot is on the south side of the line to Chester, about 1¼ miles west of Crewe station, and is partially visible from the line.

Walking directions: Turn left outside the station along Nantwich Road, and right at the traffic lights into Mill Street. Continue under the railway bridge, turning left into Oak Street, going on into Wistaston Road. The depot entrance is on the right-hand side of this road ¾ mile further on. Walking time 30min.

Below:
Crewe Electric Depot, which is currently home for the Class 85 fleet as well as EMUs of Class 304, consists of a 4-track through shed with undercover accommodation for approximately 16 locomotives. In common with CD, CE also undertakes recommissioning of traction released from the adjacent BREL Works. This illustration taken in 1961 shows a selection of Classes 81 and 82 stabled in and around the depot. *BR*

CARDIFF CANTON

Location No: 78520 (Loco), 78521 (DMU)
Region: Western
Gazetteer Ref: 43 B 5
Original Codes: 86A, 86C
Type of Depot: TMD
Exam Code: E, Unit

Classes Allocated: 08, 37, 47, 56, 101, 108, 110, 115, 116, 117, 119, 150, CS
Duties Performed: Local shunting, local/main line passenger and freight
Notes: Wheel lathe. 4×Snowploughs. BTU

The depot is on the south side of the main Cardiff-Swansea line west of Cardiff station, and is visible from the line.

Walking directions: Turn left outside Cardiff Central station into Central Square, turn left into Wood Street, and cross the river bridge. Continue into Tudor Street and then along Ninian Park Road. Turn left into a cul-de-sac, and at the end a footbridge leads to the depot. Walking time 15min.

Below:
Motive power resources for Cardiff and South Wales are provided by the sizeable Canton depot, west of Cardiff station. The complex consists of one large maintenance building with both east- and west-facing access, with a separate service and fuelling building supplemented by a number of stabling sidings. This view shows the depot looking west, with the heavy maintenance shop on the left and the service depot in the centre.   *David Nicholas*

On arrival at CF, locomotives pass through the fuelling and service depot. If all is in order the locomotive is released for its next duty, but if problems are found the machine goes to the repair depot or factory. Class 47/0 No 47225 in company with two Class 37s and a Class 45 are seen inside the fuel/service building in January 1983. *David Nicholas*

In mid 1986 CF's allocation consisted of 141 Class 08, 37, 47 and 56 locomotives, primarily for South Wales and inter-regional passenger/freight duties. This view of the west end of the maintenance depot is one that cannot be seen every day with Class 73/1 No 73123, Class 33/0 No 33008, Class 40 No 40122 and a Class 20 occupying the yard, as exhibits at the 1985 Open Day. *Colin J. Marsden*

CHESTER

Location No: 40304
Region: Midland
Gazetteer Ref: 20 D 4
Original Codes: 6A
Type of Depot: TMD
Exam Code: A, Unit

Classes Allocated: 100, 101, 108, 116, 120
Duties Performed: Local shunting, North Wales passenger services
Notes: Depot also maintains main line traction

The depot is on the east side of the Upton-by-Chester line, north of the station, and is visible from the line.

Walking directions: Turn right outside the station into Station Road, and ascend a flight of steps on the right side, turn right into Hoole Way, and the entrance to the depot is a private road on the left, just after the railway crossing. Walking time 5min.

Below:
Chester is basically a DMU depot today. The depot consists of a covered servicing depot with fuel and stabling sidings outside. In addition to maintaining its own allocation the depot gives service examinations to main line traction. This illustration of the depot interior taken on 6 October 1979 shows Class 104 set No 50540/56175. *David Nicholas*

TOPS CODE: CR

COLCHESTER

Location No: 50048
Region: Eastern
Gazetteer Ref: 12 E 4
Original Codes: 30E
Type of Depot: SD
Exam Code: B
Classes Allocated:

Duties Performed: Local shunting
Notes: Depot also maintains main line traction and stables EMU/DMU stock.
2×Snowploughs

The depot is on the west side of the London-Colchester line, south of the station, and is visible from the line and station platforms.

Walking directions: Turn left outside the station, and a path leads to the depot from a small gate in the fence. Walking time 5min.

Below:
Colchester depot, located opposite the up platform at Colchester station, has a shed with two through roads containing fuel and replenishment supplies for all locomotive classes operating in the area. Stabling sidings are located at either end and behind the depot building. Class 47/0 No 47099 is seen stabled outside the east end of the depot on 25 February 1984. *Colin J. Marsden*

CRICKLEWOOD

Location No: 63402
Region: Midland
Gazetteer Ref: 39 B 4
Original Codes: 14A
Type of Depot: TMD
Exam Code: E, Unit

Classes Allocated: 317, CS
Duties Performed: Local shunting, freight and St Pancras-Bedford passenger

The depot is on the east side of the line, north of the station, and is visible from the line.

Walking directions: Turn left outside the station into Cricklewood Lane, and first left into Claremont Road, turn left again into Brent Terrace, and the depot entrance is on the left side. Walking time 10min.

Cricklewood depot closed to locomotive activity in spring 1987.

Below:
The depot at Cricklewood has considerably expanded over recent years, following electrification of the Bedford-St Pancras line and general modernisation of the MR routes. Locomotive fuel and service facilities are provided at the Cricklewood station end of the depot, while EMU facilities are at the Mill Hill end. With the fuelling bay on the left, a line-up of Class 45s and a Class 47 are seen in the stabling sidings during October 1983. *Michael J. Collins*

DONCASTER

Location No: 23431
Region: Eastern
Gazetteer Ref: 21 F 5
Original Codes: 36A
Type of Depot: TMD
Exam Code: B

Classes Allocated: 08
Duties Performed: Local shunting
Notes: Depot also maintains main line traction. Wheel lathe. 2×Snowploughs. BTU

The depot is on the east side of the Doncaster-London line ½ mile south of the station, and is visible from the line.

Walking directions: Cross the station yard, turning half right into Station Road, continue at the end into West Street, and turn right into St Sepulchre Gate West. Cross Cleveland Street (by the overbridge), and continue until the roundabout. Here turn left into Kellam Street, and turn right into a cul-de-sac at the end. A path leads to the depot from the end of this cul-de-sac. Walking time 20min.

Below:
Doncaster depot or 'Decoy Loco' as it is known locally, has an allocation of only Class 08s but in fact a vast variety of main line classes can usually be recorded on the depot, with the most common visitors being Classes 56 and 58 off local freight traffic. Doncaster depot also plays host to most locomotives released from the nearby Doncaster Works. In this January 1981 picture Class 31/1s Nos 31317/218 stand alongside Class 37/0 No 37021 outside the north end of the depot.
Colin J. Marsden

TOPS CODE: DY

DERBY (ETCHES PARK)

Location No: 57411
Region: Midland
Gazetteer Ref: 41 G 2
Original Codes: 16C
Type of Depot: TMD
Exam Code: C, Unit
Classes Allocated: 08, 150, 151, 154, CS

Duties Performed: Local shunting, Midland passenger services

Notes: Depot also maintains main line traction, including HQ-allocated stock at the RTC

The depot is on the east side of the Derby-Nottingham line south of Derby station and is visible from the line.

Walking directions: Go straight ahead outside Derby station into Midland Road, and left at the traffic lights into London Road. Cross the railway overbridge, and continue past the Railway Technical Centre. Turn left into Deadmans Lane, and the depot entrance is just after the railway overbridge. Walking time 20min.

Below:
Derby Etches Park is primarily a DMU depot with members of Classes 150, 151 and 154 on their books. In addition, Class 08s are maintained for local yard workings as well as shunting at the two nearby BREL Works. One of the prototype BR Class 150 DMUs No 150001 is seen protruding from the depot in this April 1986 illustration. In addition to unit and shunter stock, DY sees a number of main line locomotives and often plays host to locomotives arriving or departing from Derby Locomotive Works. *John Tuffs*

EDINBURGH (CRAIGENTINNY)

Location No: 04521
Region: Scottish
Gazetteer Ref: 30 B 2
Original Codes: None
Type of Depot: T&RSMD

Exam Code: Unit
Classes Allocated: 254, CS
Duties Performed: ECML passenger services

The depot is on the south side of the Prestonpans line about 2 miles east of Edinburgh station, and is visible from the line.

Walking directions: Leave Edinburgh Waverley station by the Waverley steps. Turn right at the top into Princes Street. Continue into Waterloo Place, Regent Road, Montrose Terrace and London Road, carry on for about 1 mile past Meadowbank sports stadium and continue into Portobello Road. Soon after crossing the main road, turn right into Fishwives Causeway. Bear right into a 'no through road' and cross over the railway. A path leads from the left of this road to the depot. Walking time 60min.

Bus directions: Lothian Transport Nos 12, 15, 26 and 86 operate from Princes Street to Portobello, Baileyfield Road, and the Fishwives Causeway.

Below:
Designed expressly for the maintenance of IC125 sets and conventional coaching stock, EC is located south of the City of Edinburgh and viewable from the main line. The traction allocation to the depot consists of 10 IC125 power cars and five IC125 passenger rakes. The depot is also responsible for the Edinburgh-Glasgow push-pull stock (not locomotives) and it is two rakes of this stock we see inside the depot on 23 March 1980. Note the shallow side pits provided for changing disc brake pads. *David Nicholas*

TOPS CODE: ED

EASTFIELD

Location No: 06430
Region: Scottish
Gazetteer Ref: 44 D 4
Original Codes: 65A
Type of Depot: TMD
Exam Code: E, Unit
Classes Allocated: 20, 26, 27, 37, 47, 101, 104

Duties Performed: Local shunting, main and local passenger and freight, Glasgow suburban passenger services

Notes: Wheel lathe. 2×Snowploughs. BTU. Scottie dog logo.

The depot is on the east side of the Glasgow Queen Street-Edinburgh line 2 miles north of the station, and is visible from the line.

Walking directions: Turn right out of Queen Street station into West George Street. Turn right into Dundas Street, right into Parliamentary Road, and left at the end into Castle Street. Continue along Springburn for about 1 mile, passing BREL Glasgow on the right. Turn left into Hawthorn Street, and a road on the left side just before the railway bridge leads to the depot. Walking time 45min.

Train directions: From Glasgow Queen Street: Travel on a Springburn train from Glasgow Queen Street Low Level, alighting at Springburn. Turn right outside the station into Hawthorn Street, and a drive to the right leads to the depot just before the railway bridge. Journey time 30min.

Bus directions: From Glasgow Central: Turn left outside the station into Gorden Street, turn right into Hope Street, and board a No 52 bus bound for Springburn, alighting by the railway bridge in Hawthorn Street, from where a drive leads to the depot. Journey time 35min. (NOTE: Bus service does not operate on Sunday.)

Below:
The largest motive power depot in Scotland is Eastfield with an allocation total of 133 in April 1986. The depot is fully equipped to perform all types of examination including, if necessary, major component changes. The view from the east end of the depot can be quite spectacular with the whole depot viewable from nearby public land. This panoramic shot shows Classes 08, 20, 25, 26, 27 and 47 in September 1977. *Les Nixon*

Below:
As well as maintaining its own fleet of locomotives, ED has an allocation of DMU stock and carries out repairs to other depots' traction if required. The depot is also fitted with a wheel lathe which sees an almost constant use. On 20 April 1986 Class 47/4 No 47617 is seen receiving tyre reprofiling on the lathe.   *Tom Noble*

Bottom:
ED is equipped to undertake virtually any maintenance operation and, to assist with this, certain areas of the covered accommodation are dedicated to special operations. To the side of the main depot building is the fuelling shed which when photographed on 20 April 1986, had Class 08 No 08853 receiving attention.
Tom Noble

SWL 2 TONNES

ENGINE OIL LEVELS
ON 08/03 MUST ONLY
BE CHECKED
WHEN THE ENGINES
ARE STOPPED

TOPS CODE: EH

EASTLEIGH

Location No: 86093
Region: Southern
Gazetteer Ref: 4 D 3
Original Codes: 70D, 71A, ELH, ELGI I
Type of Depot: TMD
Exam Code: E, Unit

Classes Allocated: 08, 09, 33, 204, 205
Duties Performed: Local shunting, local and main line passenger and freight. Hampshire DEMU services. 2×Snowploughs. BTU

The depot is at the end of a short spur line on the east side of the main London-Southampton line, south of the station, and is not clearly visible from the line.

Walking directions: Turn left outside Eastleigh station into the main Southampton Road. Turn first left into Campbell Road which crosses the railway, and the depot entrance is on the right-hand side after about ¼ mile. Walking time 15min.

Below:
Eastleigh diesel depot — adjacent to the BREL Works — has an allocation of locomotive Classes 08, 09, 33, together with Class 204 and 205 DEMU stock. The depot is divided into a running/service shed with a heavy maintenance repair point by the side. Both the running and maintenance section have four covered roads each. Class 33/1 No 33110 receives draw gear attention in the maintenance section on 7 July 1981. *Colin J. Marsden*

The heavy maintenance section has facilities for most classifications of depot repair, including bogie removal and power unit changes. To lift locomotive bodies clear of bogies, Matterson synchronised jacks are provided. EH-allocated Class 33/0 No 33010 is seen on the lifting jacks in this illustration, while a Class 205 DEMU receives repair in the next road. *Colin J. Marsden*

Bottom:
Whilst the heavy maintenance facility consists of a single-ended building the service shed has four through roads. All locomotives arriving at Eastleigh pass through the service shed where fuel, oil, water and sand supplies are replenished. Until 1984 there was a wheel lathe in one road (left in illustration) but this is now out of use. Some Motorail vehicle repairs are effected at this depot. Out of picture on the left are a number of storage and stabling sidings, usually used to accommodate EMU/DMU stock. Class 455 No 455828 protrudes from the wheel lathe road on 25 April 1984. *Colin J. Marsden*

TOPS CODE: EM

EAST HAM

Location No: 51602
Region: Eastern
Gazetteer Ref: 40 B 2
Original Codes: None
Type of Depot: EMUD

Exam Code: Unit
Classes Allocated: 302, 308
Duties Performed: ER (GE)
suburban passenger services

The depot is between the up and down line east of East Ham LRT station, and is visible from the line.

Walking directions: Turn left outside East Ham LRT station into High Street, and left into Burges Road, turn left into Stevenage Road where the depot entrance is to be found situated between the two bridges. Walking time 20min.

Below:
The main LT&S line service and maintenance facility is East Ham, with an allocation of Class 302 and 308 units. This fully electrified depot does not have facilities for locomotives and only limited capacity for EMU repairs, all major problems being transferred to Ilford. Taken in July 1979 this view shows Class 302s Nos 295 and 227 inside the depot. A number of uncovered stabling sidings exist between the depot and the running lines. *Michael J. Collins*

FRODINGHAM

Location No: 22043
Region: Eastern
Gazetteer Ref: 22 F 4
Original Codes: 36C
Type of Depot: SD
Exam Code: A

Classes Allocated: 08*
Duties Performed: Local shunting
Notes: Depot also carries out maintenance on main line traction

The depot is on the north side of the Scunthorpe-Grimsby line east of Scunthorpe station, and is visible from the line.

Walking directions: Turn right outside Scunthorpe station into Station Road, and at the end turn left into Briggs Road. Turn right into Dawes Road, and the depot entrance is on the right after about 100yd past the railway crossing. Walking time 20min.

* Depot lost allocation in spring 1987.

Below:
Frodingham depot in Scunthorpe is primarily a shunter depot, with an allocation of just Class 08s. However, the depot does carry out a number of service examinations principally to Classes 20, 31 and 47 operating into the Scunthorpe area on freight traffic. A Class 20 poses inside the depot building next to the fuel, oil, water and coolant supplies. *Colin J. Marsden*

FRATTON

Location No: 86323
Region: Southern
Gazetteer Ref: 4 E 2
Original Codes: 70F, 71D, FRA, FTON
Type of Depot: EMUD
Exam Code: A, Unit

Classes Allocated: 412, 421, 423, CS
Duties Performed: SR (SW) main line passenger services
Notes: Main line diesel and electric traction is also maintained at the depot

The depot is on the east side of the line just north of the station and is visible from the line.

Walking directions: Leave Fratton station by the southern exit, turn left into Goldsmith Avenue, and the depot entrance is on the left, after ¼ mile. Walking time 10min.

Below:
Fratton depot can be split into two distinct sections — the locomotive fuel/inspection point, and the EMU depot. The fuel point (illustrated) is adjacent to the station down platform and carries out the basic in-traffic service requirements and fuel replenishment to locomotives operating into the area, principally on Bristol-Portsmouth and North-South inter-regional duties. Class 33/0 No 33033 stands by the fuel equipment.   *Colin J. Marsden*

Below:
The EMU depot at Fratton, with its 1986 allocation of 55 main line units, has a
four-track shed where all routine examinations are effected. A large number of
open stabling sidings are also provided, primarily used for unit storage between
duties, and carriage cleaning. A coach washing machine is provided in the depot
exit road. Class 412 No 2307 and Class 421 No 7438 pose inside the shed on
18 June 1984.   Colin J. Marsden

Bottom:
In addition to the depot and inspection point, FR has a sizeable yard where freight,
passenger and NPCCS vehicles can be recorded. In recent years a number of
withdrawn/stored EMUs have been stabled in the yard pending scrap. In this June
1984 view various withdrawn Class 414 (2-HAP) units can be seen.
Colin J. Marsden

TOPS CODE: GD

GATESHEAD

Location No: 13240
Region: Eastern
Gazetteer Ref: 28 A 1
Original Codes: 52A
Type of Depot: TMD
Exam Code: E

Classes Allocated: 03, 08, 37, 47, 56
Duties Performed: Local shunting. Local and main line freight. Main line passenger
Notes: Wheel lathe. 4×Snowploughs. BTU

The depot is on the north side of the Greensfield Junction-Gateshead West Junction line, and is visible from the line.

Walking directions: Turn right outside Newcastle upon Tyne station into Neville Street and right into Westgate Road, turn right at the end and cross the High Level bridge, carrying on into Hudson Street. Turn right, cross under the railway, and this road leads to the depot. Walking time 20min.

Below:
Tyneside's major diesel service/repair depot is Gateshead, located south of the River Tyne. Like many of the larger depots, separate fuel/service and heavy maintenance facilities exist. This illustration shows the fuel/service shed with its two single locomotive-length bays. Behind the nearest Class 37, the depot fuel supply tanks can be seen. *Colin J. Marsden*

During 1986 the GD allocation presently consisted of 117 locomotives, made up of Classes 03, 08, 37, 47 and 56, supplying virtually all motive power requirements for the Newcastle area, including the Tyne yard complex, MGR services and main line passenger/freight operations. This illustration shows the outside of the maintenance building with various Classes 08, 37, 47 and 45 locomotives present. *Brian Morrison*

Bottom:
Gateshead maintenance depot is fully equipped to carry out all routine classified overhauls to its allocated classes; this includes major internal component changes or bogie replacement if required. Four Class 47s (No 47426 nearest the camera) are seen inside the maintenance depot on 9 June 1985. *Michael J. Collins*

GILLINGHAM

Location No: 89011
Region: Southern
Gazetteer Ref: 6 B 5
Original Codes: 73D, 73F
Type of Depot: EMU
Classes Allocated: 416

Duties Performed: SE main/suburban electrified network
Notes: Depot maintains SG allocated stock. Units of own allocation especially for Maidstone line services

The depot is on the south side of the line east of Gillingham station. Both depot and adjacent yard are visible from the line.

Walking directions: Turn left outside the station and left into Balmoral Road, at the end of the road turn left, and the entrances to the stabling and servicing depots are located on the left and right sides. Walking time 5min.

Below:
Such is the complexity of the SR suburban network, a large number of significant depots exist in a comparatively small area, one of the most recent to gain its own allocation is Gillingham which has sizeable covered accommodation and an allocation of Class 416/4 units for Paddock Wood-Strood line services. This general view inside the shed shows a Network SouthEast 4VEP No 7835 sharing depot space with GI allocated EPB No 6407. *Brian Morrison*

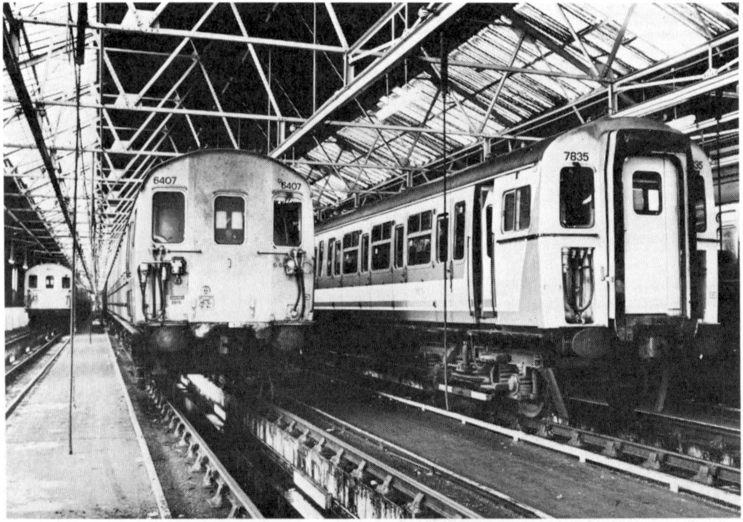

TOPS CODE: GL

GLOUCESTER

Location No: 68101
Region: Western
Gazetteer Ref: 9 E 3
Original Codes: 85B
Type of Depot: SD
Exam Code: A

Classes Allocated: 08, 97
Duties Performed: Local shunting
Notes: Depot also maintains main line traction

The depot is on the north side of the Gloucester-Birmingham line east of the station, and is visible from the platforms and line.

Walking directions: Turn right outside the station, and right again into a subway leading under the station. Turn right into Great Western Road, and right again into Horton Road. The depot entrance is on the right just before the level crossing. Walking time 15min.

Below:
To assist with motive power requirements in the Gloucester area a small depot is sited opposite Gloucester station. The actual paper allocation is confined to four Class 08 and two departmental shunters, but in practice main line traction will inevitably be seen at the depot. This illustration shows the depot as seen from the station. *Brian Morrison*

GRANGEMOUTH

Location No: 05100
Region: Scottish
Gazetteer Ref: 30 B 4
Original Codes: 31D, 65F
Type of Depot: SD

Exam Code: C
Classes Allocated: 08*
Duties Performed: Local shunting

The depot is on a freight-only line between Falkirk and Grangemouth, and is not visible from the line.

Walking directions: From Falkirk Grahamston: Turn right outside the station into Vicar Street, and left into Weir Street. At the end of this road descend a flight of steps into Kerse Lane, and turn left. Continue into Grangemouth Road for about 1 mile. Turn right into Laurieston Road — and the depot entrance is on the left. Walking time 30min.

From Falkirk High: Turn right outside the station into High Station Road, bearing left at the end into High Street. Take the first right into Wooer Street (which is an alley), at the far end turn into Manor Street, and left into Kerse Lane — then follow the instructions above. Journey time 35min.

*   Depot lost its allocation in spring 1987.

Below:
The depot at Grangemouth, located near to Falkirk on the freight-only network, is undoubtedly retained because of the abundance of freight activity in the area. The covered shed consists of seven roads, and whilst major maintenance cannot be effected, service checks are carried out. Fuel facilities are to be found at the front of the depot and virtually all ScR-allocated classes are regular visitors. Class 37/0 No 37157 and Class 27/2 No 27206 are seen at the depot on 10 August 1982.
John Tuffs

TOPS CODE: GW

GLASGOW SHIELDS

Location No: 07202
Region: Scottish
Gazetteer Ref: 44 E 3
Original Codes: None
Type of Depot: ETMD
Exam Code: J, Unit

Classes Allocated: 81, 303, 311, 314, 318
Duties Performed: Glasgow suburban passenger. ECML passenger and freight
Notes: Wheel lathe. Salmon logo

The depot is on the south side of the Glasgow Central-Paisley line, 1 mile west of Glasgow Central station.

Travel directions: From Glasgow Central: From the Union Street exit turn right into Union Street, turn left into Argyle Street, and right again into St Enoch Square. From here travel by Glasgow Underground to Shields Road station. Outside turn right into Scotland Street, left into Shields Road, and right into St Andrews Drive, the depot entrance being on the left. Journey time 30min.

From Glasgow Queen Street: Depart the station into Buchanan Street Underground station, take the Underground service to Shields Road station, and continue as above. Journey time 30min.

Below:
In collaboration with the Glasgow-Gourock/Wemyss Bay electrification, a four-road electric depot was built at Glasgow Shields Road to provide maintenance facilities for the EMU fleet. However today, with the WCML electrification, the depot is more widely used, and is home for the Class 81 fleet and, up until late-1985, the Class 370 APT. A number of vehicle/unit storage sidings are provided adjacent to the shed (left in picture).   *BR*

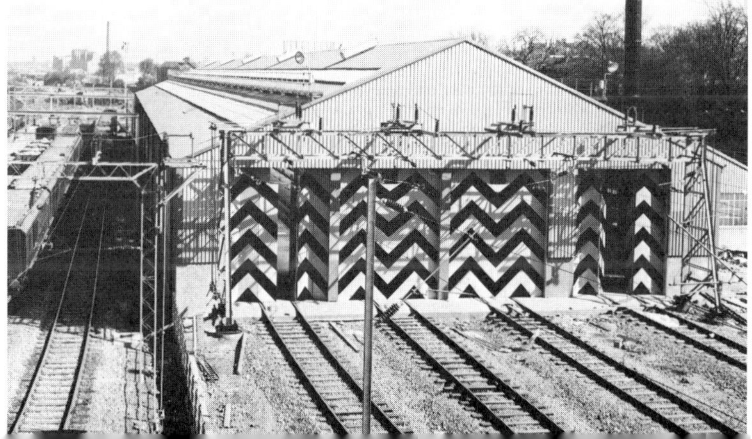

HAYMARKET

Location No: 04230
Region: Scottish
Gazetteer Ref: 30 G 3
Original Codes: 64B
Type of Depot: TMD
Exam Code: E, Unit

Classes Allocated: 08, 20, 26, 47, 101, 110, 120
Duties Performed: Local shunting, Edinburgh suburban passenger, ECML passenger/freight
Notes: Wheel lathe. BTU. Castle logo

The depot is on the north side of the Glasgow and Fife lines west of Haymarket station, and is visible from the line.

Walking directions: Turn left outside Haymarket station into Haymarket Terrace, and continue along this road for about 1 mile. Turn sharp left into Russell Road just after a railway bridge. A drive leads to the depot entrance from the right-hand side of this road. Walking time 15min.

Below:
The second largest Scottish depot is Haymarket, located north of Edinburgh, on the east side of the line, where examples of Classes 08, 20, 26, 27 and 47 are housed. The depot is again separated into a service and repair side. This illustration shows the south end of the complex, with the service section in the middle, and the repair area to the right.   *David Nicholas*

Below:
On the east side of the maintenance building a small corrugated steel-built repair shop is provided, where heavy maintenance and lifting is carried out. Standing at the north end of this building, Class 26 No 26011 posed for the camera on 14 April 1983.   *David Nicholas*

Bottom:
The lifting shop at HA is fully equipped to undertake all classified overhauls A-E on Classes 08, 20, 26, 27 and 47, as well as unit stock. Usually exams are effected only to the depot's own allocation; however, foreign motive power is repaired if the need arises. On 16 June 1983 Class 26/0 No 26010 receives a bogie overhaul while a depot fitter attends to the underside of a Class 101 diesel unit.   *John Chalcraft*

TOPS CODE: HE

HORNSEY

Location No: 54208
Region: Eastern
Gazetteer Ref: 40 A 5
Original Codes: 34B
Type of Depot: EMUD
Exam Code: Unit

Classes Allocated: 97, 312, 313, 317
Duties Performed: ER (GN) inner and outer suburban passenger
Notes: Wheel lathe

The depot is on the east side of the line, south of the station.

Walking directions: Leave Hornsey station by the footbridge, and the depot entrance is immediately afterwards on the right. Walking time 5min.

Below:
With the introduction of electric suburban services on the ER(GN) section came the construction of a sizeable EMU depot at Hornsey, where all except works category overhauls could be carried out. To keep stock in a clean external condition an automated coach washing plant was installed, seen being passed through by Class 313 No 313001. *BR*

Below:
The electrified purpose-built train shed has deep underside inspection pits on all roads, and side disc brake changing pits on the majority of roads. 'Platform' height catwalks are provided by most stabling roads enabling fitting and cleaning staff easy access. A Class 312 and three Class 313s are seen inside the depot in May 1976 soon after the opening.   *BR*

Bottom:
More heavy or routine maintenance can also be carried out at Hornsey, including tyre reprofiling. This illustration shows two synchronised screw jacks being positioned on the lifting lugs of a Class 312 unit. Note the deep pit enables the fitter to work at normal stance under the set.   *BR*

TOPS CODE: HM

HEALEY MILLS

Location No: 18421
Region: Eastern
Gazetteer Ref: 42 C 3
Original Codes: 55C
Type of Depot: SD
Exam Code: A

Classes Allocated: 08*
Duties Performed: Local shunting
Notes: Depot also maintains main line traction.
2×Snowploughs

The depot is situated in the marshalling yard complex 4 miles east of Wakefield Kirkgate.

Bus directions: From Wakefield Westgate: Travel on a West Riding/Yorkshire Traction No 261 bus bound for Huddersfield, or a West Riding No 458 for Overton, from outside Westgate station and alight at Horbury Bridge. Cross the road into Storrs Hill Road and a drive leads to the depot from the left-hand side, after the railway bridge. Journey time 35min.

From Wakefield Kirkgate: Cross the station forecourt and turn left; after crossing the main road board one of the regular buses to Wakefield bus station. Here change to a No 261 or 458 and proceed as above. Journey time 45-50min.

* Depot lost its allocation spring 1987.

Below:
One of the country's most important freight yards is Healey Mills, now only a shadow of its former size. Almost in the middle of the yard is HM depot which until the early 1980s held a main line allocation and was a thriving maintenance depot. Main line traction is still prolific at the depot with machines receiving fuel and service checks. In this view of the depot, Classes 37, 47 and 56 can be seen.
David Nicholas

HALL ROAD

Location No: 36067
Region: Midland
Gazetteer Ref: 45 F 3
Original Codes: None
Type of Depot: TMD

Exam Code: Unit
Classes Allocated: 507
Duties Performed: Liverpool suburban passenger

The depot is on the west side of the line adjacent to the station, and is visible from the line.

Walking directions: The depot entrance is on the right just outside the station. Walking time 3min.

Below:
The home for the 33 members of Class 507 is Hall Road, located on the Liverpool suburban network on the Southport route. The depot consists of two tracks adjacent to the station with a number of open air storage sidings alongside, all of which are third rail electrified. Whilst the depot carries out most routine repairs to the stock, any major overhauls are usually referred to Birkenhead. This general view of the depot was taken in April 1980. *Fred Kerr*

TOPS CODE: HT

HEATON

Location No: 12714
Region: Eastern
Gazetteer Ref: 28 A 1
Original Codes: 52B
Type of Depot: T&RSMD
Exam Code: Unit

Classes Allocated: 101, 108, 111, 143, 254, CS
Duties Performed: Local suburban passenger, ECML passenger

The depot is 2 miles north of Manors station, on the east side of the line, and is visible from the line.

Travel directions: Travel by Tyne & Wear Metro service to Walkergate. Turn left outside the station, and the depot entrance is on the left by the railway bridge. Walking time 5min.

Below:
Maintenance and repair facilities have existed at Heaton for many years, but in collaboration with the introduction of IC125s on ECML duties a new purpose-built facility was erected in 1975/77. The depot is able to undertake all IC125 and DMU repairs to stock operating in the northeast. In addition to covered accommodation a number of open air sidings are provided. In this view we see the main depot with, from left to right, the servicing, maintenance and bogie cleaning shops.   *BR*

ILFORD

Location No: 50422
Region: Eastern
Gazetteer Ref: 40 B 1
Original Codes: None
Type of Depot: ETMD

Exam Code: Unit
Classes Allocated: 302, 305, 306, 307, 308, 315, CS
Duties Performed: ER (GE) suburban main line services

The depot is on the north side of the line east of the station, and is partly visible from the line.

Walking directions: Turn left outside the station, then right into Ley Street, and the depot entrance is on the right. Walking time 5min.

Below:
The largest of the ER EMU servicing/repair depots is Ilford, where a sprawling complex of stabling, repair and carriage cleaning shops are to be found. IL is currently responsible for 170 EMU sets; additionally it carries out repairs to coaching stock vehicles and keeps an eye on the 25kV Class 86s operating on ER(GE) duties. Our illustration shows a line-up of Classes 307, 305 and 315 stock in August 1984. *Michael J. Collins*

IMMINGHAM

Location No: 21210
Region: Eastern
Gazetteer Ref: 22 E 2
Original Codes: 40B
Type of Depot: TMD
Exam Code: E

Classes Allocated: 08, 20, 31, 37, 47
Duties Performed: Local shunting, Humberside freight diagrams
Notes: 2×Snowploughs

The depot is in the Dockland area, on the north side of the Ulceby-Grimsby Dock line, which is not usually used by passenger services.

Bus directions: Board a Lincolnshire Transport No 45 bus bound for Immingham in Bethlehem Street, adjacent to Grimsby Town station, and alight at the depot entrance in Queens Road, Immingham. Journey time 30min.

Below:
Positioned in the freight-only complex of Immingham Docks on South Humberside, IM's main brief is to supply motive power for the mass of freight activity in the area. Forty ETH-fitted Class 31s being mainly deployed on trans-Pennine duties are also allocated to the depot. In this July 1981 illustration the following locomotives can be seen: 37160, 37226, 47236, 31124 and 08439.
Michael J. Collins

INVERNESS

Location No: 01113
Region: Scottish
Gazetteer Ref: 36 E 5
Original Codes: 32A, 60A
Type of Depot: TMD
Exam Code: E
Classes Allocated: 08, 37, 47 CS

Duties Performed: Local shunting, Scottish and ECML passenger and freight
Notes: 2×Snowploughs. 1×Snowblower. Stag Logo

The depot is in the triangle of lines at the east end of the station and is visible from the line and station.

Walking directions: A boarded crossing leads from the east end of Platform 5 to the depot. Walking time 5min.

Below:
The most northerly traction depot in Great Britain is Inverness which has an allocation of Classes 08, 37 and 47, usually deployed on Inverness-Kyle, Wick, Thurso, Aberdeen and Glasgow duties. The depot is basically as built by the Highland Railway but, of course, now contains modern equipment. In 'more yellow' livery Class 37/0 No 37264 stands outside the depot in November 1984.
Colin J. Marsden

A corrugated steel shrouded locomotive fuel point is located adjacent to the station-avoiding line and can accommodate two locomotives at one time. Usually when locomotives arrive 'on depot' they first pass through the fuel area prior to undergoing repairs or internal exams. Class 26/1 Nos 26041/034 are seen on the fuel point. The fuel supply tanks are behind the locomotives. *Colin J. Marsden*

CARLISLE (KINGMOOR)

Location No: 09151
Region: Midland
Gazetteer Ref: 26 C 1
Original Codes: 12A
Type of Depot: TMD
Exam Code: E
Classes Allocated: 08, 31, 40, 47, 108

Duties Performed: Local shunting, Cumbria passenger and freight, WCML passenger/freight

Notes: Depot also maintains 25kV ac electric locomotives. 4×Snowploughs. BTU

The depot is on the west side of the main line about 1½ miles north of Carlisle station, and is visible from the line.

Bus directions: From the station go ahead into Court Square, turn left into English Street, and then into Scotch Street. From here travel on a Ribble No 663 or 664 bus alighting at Etterby Scaur, walk along Etterby Road, cross the railway and the depot entrance is on the right. Travel time 35min.

Below:
Situated in the sizeable yard complex north of Carlisle is Kingmoor depot. The main covered shed building has six roads which is complemented by many storage and stabling sidings. In this view taken in 1983 various members of Classes 25 and 40, together with DMUs and breakdown train vehicles, can be seen. *David Nicholas*

Left:
There are a wide range of maintenance facilities provided at IS including synchronised Matterson jacks enabling bodies to be lifted clear of bogies for removal. Two roads of the shed building are dedicated to heavy repair work, while another two are used for service checks and daily overhauls. Snowplough-fitted Class 47/4 No 47541 *The Queen Mother* is seen lifted in one of the maintenance roads. *Colin J. Marsden*

Below:
Now withdrawn Class 25/0 No 25033 stands with Scottish-allocated Class 27
No 27024 outside the depot in August 1982, with a Class 108 standing inside the
depot. Most roads are equipped with 25kV ac overhead power lines.   *Fred Kerr*

KNOTTINGLEY

Location No: 18018
Region: Eastern
Gazetteer Ref: 21 E 4
Original Codes: 55G
Type of Depot: TMD
Exam Code: A

Classes Allocated: 08
Duties Performed: Local shunting
Notes: Depot also maintains main line traction

The depot is east of Knottingley station on the south side of the Goole line, and is visible from the line.

Walking directions: Leave the station by the approach road and turn right into Hill Top. Turn right into Headlands and left into Spawd Bone Lane, and the depot entrance is on the left. Walking time 10min.

Below:
KY depot, with an allocation of just four Class 08s, is one of the most important in terms of motive power and manpower for the Aire Valley MGR operations. The depot building consists of a 4-track servicing shed with fuel equipment outside. To the side of the locomotive depot (right in picture) a wagon repair depot is located dealing solely with MGR wagons. For the MGR operations KY usually deploys about eight Class 56s from the TI allocation. *Colin J. Marsden*

Left:
Kingmoor is equipped to undertake all examinations on Classes 08, 31, 40, 47 and DMUs. In addition, facilities are provided to give 'service' to a variety of visiting types such as Classes 20, 26, 27 or 45 which can be seen on the depot from time to time. In this August 1982 illustration, snowplough-fitted No 47464 undergoes routine maintenance inside the depot buildings. *Fred Kerr*

LAIRA

Location No: 84090
Region: Western
Gazetteer Ref: 1 D 5
Original Codes: 83D, 84A
Type of Depot: T&RSMD
Exam Code: E, Unit

Classes Allocated: 08, 37, 50, 118, 142, 253, CS
Duties Performed: Local shunting, WR and inter-regional passenger and freight
Notes: Wheel lathe. 2×Snowploughs

The depot is on the west side of the Newton Abbot-Plymouth line east of Plymouth station, and is visible from the line.

Walking directions: Turn left outside the station into the approach road. Turn left at the end into Glen Park Avenue, immediate right into Winston Avenue, and left into North Road East. Turn left again at the end into Laira Old Road. After about ½ mile turn right into Brandon Road (small lane). At the end of this cul-de-sac cross under the line, and the depot entrance is on the right. Walking time 45min.

Bus directions: Plymouth joint services operate from the city centre Nos 8, 20, 21, 27 and 27A pass Brandon Road. The city is only 5min walk from the station.

Below:
The responsibility for motive power operations in Devon and Cornwall falls upon Laira depot in Plymouth, where a sizeable complex exists with an allocation of shunting and main line diesel locomotives, IC125s, DMUs and locomotive-hauled stock. The depot buildings can be split into three sections — locomotive running/service, heavy maintenance and IC125 repairs. Class 50 No 50010 *Monarch* stands outside the service depot, adjacent to the fuelling equipment. *Colin J. Marsden*

Below:
Considerable modernisation was carried out at LA in the late 1970s prior to the
introduction of IC125s. This included the construction of a 3-track IC125 depot
adjacent to the locomotive facility, and alteration to a number of yard sidings to
accommodate fixed formation stock. Two Class 47s are illustrated inside the IC125
depot.   *Colin J. Marsden*

Bottom:
The most recent addition to LA's allocation are Class 142 'Skipper' railbus sets,
introduced to replace the ageing Class 118 DMMU stock. The first 'Skipper' to
arrive on the WR, No 142015, poses next to Class 47/4 No 47620 outside the
service shed; behind the Class 142 is the larger 2-track heavy repair depot.
Colin J. Marsden

TOPS CODE: LE

LANDORE

Location No: 79320
Region: Western
Gazetteer Ref: 7 B 4
Original Codes: 87A, 87E
Type of Depot: TMD
Exam Code: E
Classes Allocated: 08, 101, 119
Duties Performed: Local shunting. WR main line passenger and freight

Notes: Depot also maintains main line traction, and has a BR-operated repair shop which carries out classified repairs to other depots' motive power. Wheel lathe. 2×Snowploughs

The depot is in the fork between the Cardiff-Swansea, and Llanelli-Swansea lines, and is visible from the lines.

Walking directions: Turn right outside Swansea station into High Street, fork right into Prince of Wales Road, at the end follow the footpath into the road overbridge and into Neath Road. A drive leads to the depot from the left side, between two railway overbridges. Walking time 25min.

Below:
The major maintenance facility in West Wales is Landore (Swansea), which holds an allocation of Class 08. LE has a heavy maintenance factory which can undertake mini-works overhauls to many classes including the Class 50s and 56s. Four Class 37s and a Class 47 are seen inside the maintenance shop. Note the wide staff working platforms.   *Colin J. Marsden*

Landore's main responsibility is for the supply of Class 37s to the Railfreight sector and to providing shunting motive power for the abundance of freight sidings in the West Wales area. In addition to its own allocation of motive power, LE provides service facilities for 'foreign' locomotives operating into the area. Class 37/0 No 37279 and Class 47/0 No 47081 stand in the depot yard in January 1983. *David Nicholas*

Bottom:
Fuelling and locomotive 'service checks' are carried out in a 3-track shed at LE which is able to deal with six locomotives simultaneously. Parked inside the fuel point are two of the depot's now withdrawn Class 03s which had cut-down cabs for BPGV operation. LE is also responsible for maintenance of the three cut-down cabbed Class 08/9s. *David Nicholas*

TOPS CODE: LO (Diesel depot), LG (Electric depot)

LONGSIGHT

Location No: LO — 32511, LG — 32514
Region: Midland
Gazetteer Ref: 43 A 3
Original Codes: 9A
Type of Depot: DTMD, ETMD
Exam Code: C, J, Unit
Classes Allocated: 08, 127, 303, 304

Duties Performed: Local shunting, Manchester suburban passenger, WCML passenger/freight
Notes: The Longsight complex consists of two depots, one for diesel and the other electric

The depots are situated 1½ miles south of Manchester Piccadilly station on the east side of the Stockport line. The diesel and electric depots are adjacent, but only the yards are visible from the main line.

Walking directions: Turn left at the bottom of the Piccadilly station approach into London Road, at the roundabout go ahead into Downing Street, and into Hyde Road. The diesel depot entrance is a drive on the right after the railway overbridge. The electric depot is on the south side of the diesel depot. Walking time 35-40min.

Bus directions: From Manchester Piccadilly station board a No 94, 95, 96 or 192 bus bound for Hazel Grove, Levenshulme, or East Didsbury, and alight at the junction of Plymouth Grove, Stockport Road and Kirkmanshulme Lane. Walk down Kirkmanshulme Lane under the railway, and immediately left down a narrow alley which leads to the main depot entrances. Journey time 25min.

Two depots come under the collective title of Longsight — LG Longsight Electric, and LO Longsight Diesel. The two installations virtually merge into one, but have two distinct responsibilities. LG is responsible for the Class 304s and is also equipped to undertake 25kV electric locomotive maintenance, but since the depot lost its Class 82/83 allocation in 1984/5 few locomotives have been recorded. In this February 1983 illustration Class 85 No 85032 is seen undergoing bogie overhaul.   *David Nicholas*

Below:
LO — Longsight Diesel holds an allocation of Class 08s plus DMUs deployed on local Parcels duties; however a number of main line machines pay regular visits when working into Manchester on inter-Regional duties. In addition to the covered depot accommodation a number of stabling roads are provided, as well as full locomotive fuelling and inspection facilities. In the upper illustration Class 108 DMU No M54232 and a Class 47 are seen by the depot entrance in May 1984, while the lower plate shows Class 47/3 No 47370 and Class 31/4 No 31408 outside the depot in February 1984.   *Both: David Nicholas*

LINCOLN

Location No: 44051
Region: Eastern
Gazetteer Ref: 16 B 1
Original Codes: 40A
Type of Depot: TMD
Exam Code: A

Classes Allocated: 105, 114, CS*
Duties Performed: Local shunting, Lincolnshire/ Yorkshire passenger
Notes: 2×Snowploughs

The depot is on the south side of the Lincoln Central-Grimsby line, east of Lincoln Central. The depot is visible from the line.

Walking directions: Turn right outside Lincoln St Marks station into the approach road, and left into the High Street, turn right just after the railway crossing into St Marys Street, and proceed along this street which passes Lincoln Central station, continuing into Oxford Street. Pass under the road bridge, and into Pelham Street. After crossing the railway, descend a flight of steps and follow the path to the level crossing, from where a boarded crossing leads to the depot. Walking time from St Marks 15min, from Central 10min.

* Depot officially lost its allocation in spring 1987, but at the time of writing some DMU stock is still allocated, scheduled for closure.

Below:
Lincoln is one of the smaller maintenance depots, but nevertheless is an important link in the provincial services sector. There is one main 3-road depot building together with outside stabling sidings. A Class 114 and a Class 03 (not now allocated to the depot) pose inside the shed in July 1981.   *Michael J. Collins*

TOPS CODE: LR

LEICESTER

Location No: 59239
Region: Midland
Gazetteer Ref: 16 F 3
Original Codes: 15A
Type of Depot: SD
Classes Allocated: 08

Duties Performed: Local shunting
Notes: Depot also maintains main line traction.
2×Snowploughs

The depot is located on the east side of the Leicester-Derby line north of the station, and is visible from the line.

Walking directions: Turn left outside Leicester station into London Road and first left into Conduit Street. Turn right at the end into Sparkenhoe Street and continue into Maidstone Street. Then turn left into Beal Street and a drive leads to the depot at the end of this street. Walking time 15min.

Below:
To the north of Leicester station is Leicester depot which officially has only an allocation of two Class 08s. However, in practice a number of main line locomotives will usually be found. Only routine service checks, fuel etc can be provided at this location, and for major repairs locomotives have to be returned to their home depot. This general view of the stabling point/depot from the nearby overbridge shows various members of Classes 47, 31, 56, 45 and 20.
Michael J. Collins

MARYLEBONE

Location No: 63021
Region: Midland
Gazetteer Ref: 39 C 5
Original Codes: 1D
Type of Depot: TMD

Exam Code: Unit
Classes Allocated: 108, 115
Duties Performed: Local passenger

The depot is on the east side of the line just north of the station, and is visible from the line.

Walking directions: From Marylebone station turn left into Boston Place, turn right into Taunton Place, sharp left into Rossmore Road, and the depot entrance is on the right. Walking time 10min.

The depot is scheduled for closure.

Below:
The only main line depot located at a London terminus is Marylebone, where a 6-road shed plus outside stabling sidings are provided. The allocation consists of Class 108 and 115 DMU stock with rare appearances by main line traction. ME is often host to main line steam locomotives involved in the running of specials between Marylebone and Stratford-upon-Avon. A general view of the north end of the depot is shown. *Brian Morrison*

MOTHERWELL

Location No: 07452
Region: Scottish
Gazetteer Ref: 44 B 2
Original Codes: 28A, 66B
Type of Depot: TMD
Exam Code: E

Classes Allocated: 08, 20, 37
Duties Performed: Local shunting, South Scottish freight
Notes: BTU. Salmon logo

The depot is on the west side of the Motherwell-Coatbridge line, north of the station, and is visible from the line.

Walking directions: Turn left outside the station along Muir Street, and a rough path leads to the depot through derelict land on the right-hand side, just after crossing the railway underbridge. Walking time 10min.

Below:
Motherwell depot, located south of Glasgow, is ideally placed for the abundance of freight traffic in the area, particularly associated with BSC workings. The depot's 1986 allocation consists of Classes 08s, 20s and 37s. Full servicing and maintenance facilities exist at the depot, but some repairs are transferred to Eastfield. In this April 1983 illustration Class 37/0s Nos 37139/152 are seen.
David Nicholas

TOPS CODE: MR

MARCH

Location No: 46203
Region: Eastern
Gazetteer Ref: 17 F 3
Original Codes: 31B
Type of Depot: TMD
Exam Code: E

Classes Allocated: 08, 31, 37
Duties Performed: Shunting, East Anglian freight and passenger
Notes: BTU

The depot is on a spur on the west side of the Wisbech line north of the station.

Walking directions: Turn left outside the station and left over the level crossing. Turn first left into Norwood Road, and at the end right into Hundred Road. A drive leads to the depot from the right-hand side. Walking time 20min.

Below:
One of the most important Cambridgeshire/East Anglian diesel depots is March, which once served the thriving March/Whitmore yards. Today the depot, with its allocation of Classes 08, 31 and 37 locomotives, supplies motive power for local/main line freight operations, and some passenger work, principally the East Anglia-Birmingham inter-regionals. There are full servicing and heavy maintenance facilities at MR. Two Class 31s and two Class 37s are seen in the depot yard. *Colin J. Marsden*

NORWICH CROWN POINT

Location No: 48221
Region: Eastern
Gazetteer Ref: 18 F 3
Original Codes: 32A
Type of Depot: TMD
Exam Code: A, Unit

Classes Allocated: 03, 08, 101, 105, CS
Duties Performed: Shunting, East Anglian local passenger services
Notes: Depot also maintains main line traction. 2×Snowploughs

The depot is on the south side of the Swing Bridge Junction to Wensum Junction line, south of the station, and is visible from the line.

Walking directions: Cross the station forecourt, and turn right into Thorpe Road, turn right again into Lower Clarence Road, and right into Clarence Road. After crossing the bridge turn left into Hardy Road, at the end of this road go through the factory gates (this is a public right of way) and turn left next to the river, pass under the railway bridge, and the depot entrance is on the left. Walking time 15min.

Below:
Another depot commissioned in the 1980s is Norwich Crown Point, which has an allocation of locomotive Classes 03 and 08 together with DMU and coaching stock vehicles. Full maintenance facilities exist for coaches and unit stock but only limited locomotive operations can be carried out. In this view a Class 03 stands outside the depot, while Class 31/4 No 31412 stands by the fuelling equipment.
David Nicholas

TOPS CODE: NH

NEWTON HEATH

Location No: 31300
Region: Midland
Gazetteer Ref: 45 A 2
Original Codes: 9D
Type of Depot: TMD
Exam Code: B, Unit
Classes Allocated: 104, 108, 142, 150

Duties Performed: Shunting, Manchester Area local passenger services
Notes: Depot also maintains main line traction.
1 × Snowplough

The depot is situated in the fork of the Miles Platting-Dean Lane, and Miles Platting-Moston lines, 2¼ miles east of Manchester Victoria station. The depot is partially visible from the line.

Bus directions (from Manchester Victoria): Turn left outside the station into Todd Street, turn right into Corporation Street, left into Cannon Street and then right into Oldham Street. From here travel on a Greater Manchester PTE No 77 bus bound for Moston, alighting at Dean Lane. The depot entrance being in this road on the left. Journey time 30min.

Below:
The most important DMU depot in the Manchester area is Newton Heath, with an allocation of Class 104, 108, 142 and 150 vehicles. The depot consists of one main shed with numerous stabling sidings and can carry out virtually any unit repair. This general view of the depot and surrounding sidings taken in April 1983, shows a Class 25 moving off the depot with various DMU sets in the yard.
David Nicholas

Below:

In addition to unit stock allocation, NH also carries out fuelling and service checks to main line diesel traction. However, heavy repairs are carried out at the locomotive's owning depot. This view shows Class 47/0 No 47104 outside the 2-track fuelling shed, while Class 25/3 No 25235 and Class 45/0 No 45034 are stabled adjacent to the depot building. *David Nicholas*

Bottom:

Today Newton Heath is responsible for Class 142 Pacer railbuses; this has, of course, been reflected in a number of conventional sets being withdrawn or reallocated. The new sets have meant that new maintenance techniques have had to be learnt, and much retraining of depot and operational staff has taken place. Painted in Greater Manchester orange livery, Class 142 No 142006 poses outside the depot on 26 April 1986. *Fred Kerr*

TOPS CODE: NL

NEVILLE HILL

Location No: 17115
Region: Eastern
Gazetteer Ref: 42 A 3
Original Codes: 55H
Type of Depot: TMD
Exam Code: E, Unit

Classes Allocated: 08, 101, 108, 110, 111, 141, 142, 144, 150, 254, CS
Duties Performed: Shunting, local and ECML passenger services

The depot is on the north side of the York line, east of Leeds station, and is partially visible from the line.

Walking directions: Turn left outside Leeds station into the approach road, and turn right into Boar Lane. Continue along Duncan Street, and fork left into Call Lane. Cross Kirkgate into New York Street, and continue into York Street. At the flyover turn right into York Road, and continue for just over 1 mile. Turn right into Osmondthorpe Lane, and the depot entrance is on the right, just before the railway overbridge. Walking time 45min.

Bus directions: Take a No 6 West Yorkshire PTE Metro Bus bound for Halton Moor which operates from outside the station, and alight at the depot entrance. Journey time 10min.

Below:
Since the introduction of diesel railcars in Yorkshire a modern traction servicing depot has been located north of Leeds at Neville Hill, but with the introduction of IC125 stock in the early 1970s, considerable modernisation was effected in 1979 when a 2-road 825ft long service depot and a 2-road 420ft long coaching stock depot were added, together with additional storage sidings. Today, in addition to DMU stock, NL has the responsibility for Class 08s and IC125 power cars with associated trailers. This aerial view shows the late 1960 additions to the depot.
BR

TOPS CODE: OC

OLD OAK COMMON

Location No: 73220
Region: Western
Gazetteer Ref: 39 C 4
Original Codes: 81A
Type of Depot: TMD
Exam Code: E

Classes Allocated: 08, 31, 47, 50, 101, 104
Duties Performed: Local shunting, local and WR main line passenger and freight
Notes: 2×Snowploughs. BTU.

The depot is on the north side of the Reading and High Wycombe lines and is not completely visible from the line.

Walking directions: From Willesden Junction station turn right into the station access road and right into Old Oak Lane, after about ¾ mile, turn left into Old Oak Common Lane, and a drive leads to the depot from the left. Walking time 15min.

Below:
The WR London Division motive power and rolling stock depot is Old Oak Common. The depot is split into several major areas: 1 Repair 'factory'. 2 Fuel and service depot. 3 Turntable. 4 Carriage sidings and, 5, IC125 depot — classified separately as 00. The main 'factory' or Heavy Maintenance Shop has six roads, each able to accommodate one locomotive. There is a double length road in the centre of the factory equipped with eight screw jacks for locomotive body lifting. Green Class 50 No 50007 *Sir Edward Elgar* is seen in the lifting bay.
Colin J. Marsden

Below:
Although the Old Oak Common IC125 allocation have their own maintenance facilities (OO) and fuel positions, any major power car repairs are effected in the 'Factory'. OC can carry out virtually any overhaul to IC125 power cars or locomotives, including bogie replacement, power unit changes etc. An IC125 power car, with the engine room inspection covers open, is seen in the 'Factory'. *Colin J. Marsden*

Bottom:
To the rear of the fuel point and 'Factory' is a turntable where a number of locomotives stand ready for their next turn of duty. Most turntable-fed roads can accommodate one main line or two shunting locomotives. In 1986 OC held an allocation of locomotives of Classes 08, 31, 47 and 50. Two Class 50 Nos 50038 *Formidable* and 50009 *Conqueror* pose in turntable stabling roads in September 1985.   *Colin J. Marsden*

OLD OAK COMMON HST

Location No: 73225
Region: Western
Gazetteer Ref: 39 C 4
Original Codes: None
Type of Depot: HSTMD

Exam Code: Unit
Classes Allocated: 253
Duties Performed: WR IC125 services

Take the same directions as for Old Oak Common, as far as Old Oak Common Lane, and continue along this road for a further ½ mile. The depot entrance is on the left. Walking time (from Willesden Junction) 20min.

Below:
The IC125 depot at Old Oak Common is coded OO and consists of a 3-track covered shed. When built in the early 1970s it was designed to hold 2+7 IC125 formations; by the mid-1980s, with the intention to strengthen IC125 sets, the shed was extended. Each of the three roads has under and side pits, and at positions convenient to power cars, all technical requirements are available. Set No 253004 is seen inside the depot on 1 February 1982.   *Colin J. Marsden*

TOPS CODE: PM

ST PHILIPS MARSH

Location No: 81524
Region: Western
Gazetteer Ref: 3 A 2
Original Codes: None
Type of Depot: HSTMD

Exam Code: Unit
Classes Allocated: 253, CS
Duties Performed: WR IC125 services

The depot is on the north side of the Bristol West Junction-North Somerset Junction line, and is not visible from any passenger line.

Walking directions: Leave Bristol Temple Meads station by the approach road, and turn left at the end into Temple Gate, continue into Bath Road (which passes Bath Road depot), and left over Totterdown bridge. Turn right into Albert Road, and the depot entrance is on the right just after the railway bridge. Walking time 25min.

Below:
With the approach of the IC125 age, major modernisation of Bristol St Philips Marsh depot took place which hitherto had been used solely for the overhaul/service of DMU stock. A new 3-road servicing/repair depot was built with associated coach-washing plant and stabling sidings. Class 253 sets Nos 253001/010 are seen at the 'new' depot in August 1976. *Graham Scott-Lowe*

TOPS CODE: PZ

PENZANCE

Location No: 85731
Region: Western
Gazetteer Ref: 1 F 4
Original Codes: 83G, 84D
Type of Depot: SD
Exam Code: A, Unit

Classes Allocated: 08, CS
Duties Performed: Shunting
Notes: Depot also maintains main line locomotives and IC125 stock

The depot is situated on the north side of the line 1¼ miles east of Penzance station at Long Rock.

Walking directions: Leave the station and turn right along East Terrace towards the heliport, continue to the roundabout, bear right for Marazion and the depot entrance is on the right after about 1 mile. Walking time 25min.

Below:
The depot at Penzance — located at Long Rock — has an allocation of just one Class 08, used for depot and station pilot duties; however, an IC125 depot and a sizeable carriage siding are also provided. The 1970s-built IC125 area consists of a single-track nine vehicle-long covered building with an adjacent siding, having canopies over the power car positions. The IC125 section is shown with sets Nos 253038/004 receiving attention. *Brian Morrison.*

TOPS CODE: RE

RAMSGATE

Location No: 89472
Region: Southern
Gazetteer Ref: 6 B 1
Original Codes: 73F, 73G, 74B, RAM, RMGT
Type of Depot: EMU

Exam Code: Unit
Classes Allocated: 411, 413, 414, 419, 423
Duties Performed: SR/Eastern section main lines

The depot is on the north side of the line adjacent to the station, and is visible from the line and station.

Walking directions: Turn right outside the station into Wilfred Road, after only a few yards turn right down a footpath parallel to the railway. At the end turn right into Newington Road and the depot entrance is on the right, just after crossing the railway. Walking time 5min.

Below:
The SR South Eastern Division main line EMU depot is Ramsgate. This depot, which only carries out maintenance to electric units, is quite large, having separate buildings for carriage cleaning and heavy maintenance. Class 423 (4VEP) No 7873 is shown in the stabling depot. In 1986 Ramsgate had an allocation of 215 EMUs. *Colin J. Marsden*

TOPS CODE: RG

READING

Location No: 74239
Region: Western
Gazetteer Ref: 4 A 2
Original Codes: 81D
Type of Depot: TMD
Exam Code: A, Unit
Classes Allocated: 08, 97, 101, 117, 118, 119, 120, 121, 128, 210

Duties Performed: Local shunting, local passenger
Notes: Depot also maintains main line traction and track machines

The depot is in the fork of the Reading-Newbury and Reading-Swindon lines west of Reading General station, and is visible from both lines.

Walking directions: Turn right outside Reading General station into Station Hill and continue into Tudor Road. Turn right into Caversham Road, and left into Northfield Road. At the end turn left into Swansea Road, and bear right into Cardiff Road. Turn left at the end into Cow Lane. The depot entrance is on the left, just past the railway overbridge. Walking time 20min.

Below:
The entire WR London division DMU allocation is based at Reading, which is a sizeable complex west of the station. The depot consists of covered maintenance sidings with an adjacent locomotive repair depot, which has been considerably extended in recent years to accommodate an amount of CCE plant including CCE shunter No 97650, seen here inside the depot alongside a Class 31/1 and other CCE stock.   *Colin J. Marsden*

RYDE ST JOHNS ROAD

Location No: Not allocated
Gazetteer Ref: 4 F 3
Region: Southern
Original Codes: 70H, 71F
Type of Depot: EMUD
Exam Code: Special, Unit

Classes Allocated: 97, 485, 486
Duties Performed: Isle of Wight 'RydeRail' services
Notes: The Class 97 is often stabled at Sandown

The depot is situated on the east side of the line next to Ryde St Johns Road station and is visible from the line.

Walking directions: Turn right outside the station, cross the railway, and the depot entrance is on the left-hand side. Walking time 5min.

Below:
The unique and isolated Isle of Wight Railway network, with its five 5-VEC and two 2-TIS sets has depot and small workshop facilities adjacent to Ryde St Johns Road station. The depot consists of a 2-track repair shop with outside siding/storage space. This general view of the depot shows its relationship to the station, the tall building in the centre being the repair shop. *Colin J. Marsden*

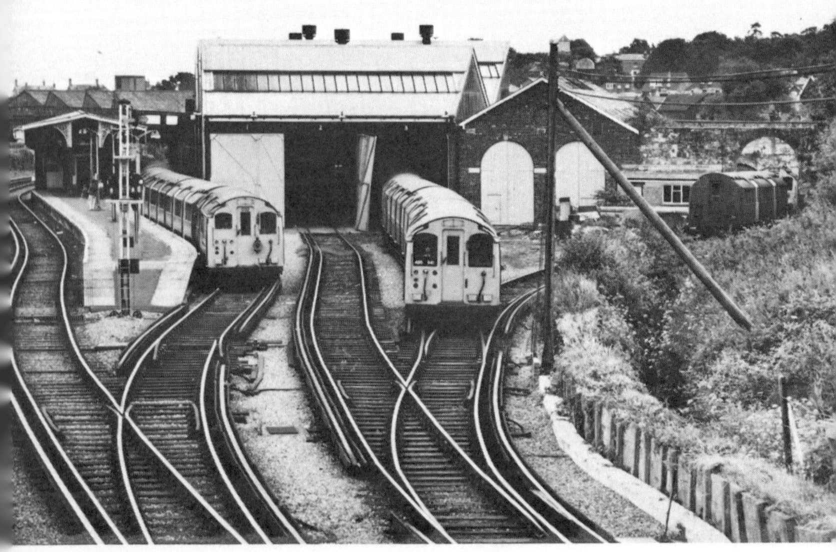

All categories of vehicle repair have to be undertaken in the comparatively small depot building as on no occasion since the electrification of the line in the mid-1960s has any stock been removed to the mainland for attention. In recent years significant modernisation has been carried out to the Island stock which has been a credit to the depot staff. The upper illustration shows a driving car of set 485041 standing inside the shop after receiving a facelift. The lower shows set 045 stabled in the yard.   *Both: Colin J. Marsden*

TOPS CODE: SB

SHIREBROOK

Location No: 28101
Region: Eastern
Gazetteer Ref: 41 C 4
Original Codes: 41J
Type of Depot: SD
Exam Code: B

Classes Allocated: 08*
Duties Performed: Local shunting
Notes: Depot also maintains main line traction.
2×Snowploughs

The depot is on the west side of the line adjacent to the closed Shirebrook West station.

Bus directions: From Alfreton & Mansfield Parkway: From the station board a Trent No 240, 241, 242, 243 or 247 bus bound for Mansfield, and alight at the terminus. Here board an East Midlands No 73B bus bound for Shirebrook, and alight at the depot entrance. Journey time 60-70min.

From Chesterfield: From the station approach turn left into Corporation Street, turn left into St Marys Gate, and continue into Lordsmill Street, turn right into Beetweel Street, and left into the bus station. Board an East Midlands No 81 bus to Langwith or Worksop, alighting in Langwith Road, Shirebrook. Walk back to the main road, and turn left, after crossing the railway the depot entrance is on the right. Journey time 60-70min.

* Depot lost allocation in spring 1987.

Below:
Another significant depot in terms of the BR Railfreight operation is Shirebrook, located deep in the heart of the Derbyshire freight-only lines, which carries out service checks and day-to-day repairs to locomotives operating on local freight work, mainly MGR coal trains. For repairs etc a 2-road depot is provided. The depot had an allocation of three Class 08s but usually Classes 47, 56 and more recently 58s are regular visitors. In this April 1981 view two Class 56s and an 08 pose inside the depot. *Michael J. Collins*

TOPS CODE: SE

ST LEONARDS

Location No: 88282
Region: Southern
Gazetteer Ref: 6 F 5
Original Codes: 73D, SLEO
Type of Depot: TMD
Exam Code: A, Unit

Classes Allocated: 203, 205, 206, 207, 411
Duties Performed: Hastings-London route South Eastern/Central section non-electrified services
Notes: Depot also has facilities for locomotive repairs

The depot is on the north side of the Bexhill line about 1½ miles east of West St Leonards station. The depot is visible from the line.

Walking directions: Turn left outside West St Leonards station into St Vincents Road, turn right into West Hill Road, and right again into Bexhill Road, and continue for about 1 mile. Turn left into Bridge Way and the depot entrance is on the left-hand side. Walking time 30min.

Below:
The majority of the SR DEMU fleet is allocated to St Leonards depot near Hastings. There are two covered shed buildings, one facing east and the other west. The building nearest St Leonards is used primarily for unit stabling (illustrated) while the other is responsible for unit maintenance and repair work. In addition to the overhauling of unit stock, SE also carries out selected repairs to Class 33s including power unit replacement. *Colin J. Marsden*

TOPS CODE: SF/SR

STRATFORD

Location No: 52230
Region: Eastern
Gazetteer Ref: 40 B 3
Original Codes: 30A
Type of Depot: TMD
Exam Code: E, Unit
Classes Allocated: 08, 31, 37, 47
Duties Performed: Local shunting, ER (GE) local and main line passenger and freight

Notes: Adjacent to the depot is a large BR-operated workshop (Stratford DRS). This sees a large number of locomotives under repair. Wheel lathe. 2×Snowploughs. BTU. Robin logo

The depot is situated on the northwest side of Stratford station, and is partially visible from the low-level platforms.

Walking directions: Turn left outside the station into William Street, from the left side a tunnel leads under the railway to the depot. Walking time 10min.

Below:
The largest of the London diesel depots is Stratford which in 1986 had an allocation of 106 locomotives of Classes 08, 31, 37 and 47 plus a number of DMU vehicles. The depot has two main running sheds with fuelling facilities and a locomotive washing plant nearby. Many stabling sidings are also provided. Class 47/4 No 47528, Class 31/1 No 31315 and Class 37/0 No 37009 are seen outside the west-facing shed. *Colin J. Marsden*

Below:
Now identified as 'Steam Roads', the tracks of the former Jubilee shed are used as storage space for locomotives available for traffic. In addition to the locomotive service facilities there is a railcar shed for the depot's allocation of DMMUs. Class 31/1 No 31193 stands in '4 Steam' road. Note the near road has the longitudinal sleepers of a former pit. *Colin J. Marsden*

Bottom:
Adjacent to Stratford R&M depot is Stratford Diesel Repair Shop (DRS) which is a BR operated workshop capable of almost any repair including bogies, power unit changes, collision damage and tyre turning. All workshop facilities are provided including overhead cranes, pits, wheel lathe and test equipment. The DRS carries out repairs to locomotives of all depots. This 1980 view of the depot shows Class 47, Nos 4742/155/004 and Class 31 No 31281. Under BR's new maintenance agreements SF has been identified as one of the depots where major works-style overhauls can be undertaken. *Michael J. Collins*

SLADE GREEN

Location No: 88425
Region: Southern
Gazetteer Ref: 5 B 4
Original Codes: SLGN
Type of Depot: M&EED
Exam Code: Special, Unit
Classes Allocated: 97, 415, 416

Duties Performed: SR/Eastern section suburban passenger
Notes: Adjacent to the running depot is a BR-operated workshop, where most SR collision and some classified exams take place. Wheel lathe

The depot is on the east side of the Dartford line south of the station and is visible from the line.

Walking directions: Turn right outside the station, and walk along a drive parallel to the railway leading to the depot. Walking time 5min.

Below:
The SR South Eastern Division suburban EMU base is Slade Green, near Dartford, where 238 Class 415/416 units consisting of a total of 834 coaches are allocated. The main depot is located on the down side of the line where a large through shed is to be found. On the opposite side of the line there are a number of stabling roads. At the far end of the EMU depot is Slade Green repair shop where most SR collision damage is rectified and classified mechanical overhauls to EMU/DMU stock carried out. *Colin J. Marsden*

TOPS CODE: SL

STEWARTS LANE

Location No: 87238
Region: Southern
Gazetteer Ref: 39 E 5
Original Codes: 73A, 75D, BAT
Type of Depot: TMD
Exam Code: E, Unit

Classes Allocated: 33, 73, 488, 489
Duties Performed: Local and main line passenger and freight
Notes: BTU

The depot is between Wandsworth Road and Battersea Park stations and is partially visible from the line.

Walking directions: From Queenstown Road station: Turn left outside the station into Queenstown Road, and follow the road round to the Queen Victoria public house, turn left into Silverthorne Road and the depot entrance is on the left after about 400yd. Walking time 10min.

Below:
The London area motive power depot on SR is Stewarts Lane, which is a sizeable complex comprising a locomotive depot, EMU servicing depot, diesel fuelling depot and stabling sidings. The main locomotive building at SL is usually referred to as the Electric Depot, being built in 1959 for the Kent Coast electrification scheme; however, today the 3-track shed is the home for diesels as well as electrics. Class 73/1s Nos 73122 *County of East Sussex* and No 73118 stand outside the depot on 12 July 1985. *Colin J. Marsden*

Below:
Inside the 'Electric Shed' there are two roads of full length, while the third can only accommodate one locomotive and is usually used for lifting. SL's allocation stands at 33 Class 33s and 47 Class 73s. To enable electrical testing of the Class 73s in the Electric depot which is not equipped with live rails, a trolley wire system is employed. Class 73s Nos 73102/005/119 stand in No 2 road on 3 June 1985 displaying InterCity, additional yellow, and rail blue liveries.
Colin J. Marsden

Bottom:
The sizeable EMU depot and associated outside sidings is home for the Gatwick Express stock. The depot also provides stabling space for SE Section EMUs and houses the VSOE Pullman stock when not in use. No live rail exists inside the EMU depot, all traction power coming from overhead trolley wires. A Gatwick Express formation, three 4-VEPs and the VSOE Pullman set are seen in the EMU depot.
Colin J. Marsden

SPRINGS BRANCH

Location No: 35150
Region: Midland
Gazetteer Ref: 45 D 2
Original Codes: 8F
Type of Depot: SD
Exam Code: E

Classes Allocated: 08
Duties Performed: Local shunting
Notes: Depot also maintains main line traction. BTU

The depot is on the east side of the West Coast main line (WCML) about 1 mile south of Wigan North Western station. The depot is visible from the line.

Walking directions: Turn right outside Wigan North Western station into Wallgate, and right into King Street. Continue into Darlington Street and fork right into Sovereign Road. Fork right again into Warrington Road, and after about 1 mile turn right into Morris Street. The depot entrance is at the end of this cul-de-sac. Walking time 30min.

Below:
Springs Branch depot in Wigan, which once boasted a main line diesel allocation, is now little more than a shunter depot, with an allocation of Class 08s. However main line traction does still use the depot, but when visited early in 1986, loco activity was at a low ebb and CCE track machines were well in evidence. In this February 1983 view of the depot Class 40 No 40152 (now withdrawn) and Class 47/4 No 47481 pose outside the 3-track shed. It is interesting to note that just one road has overhead power lines. *David Nicholas*

TOPS CODE: SU

SELHURST

Location No: 87638
Region: Southern
Gazetteer Ref: 40 G 4
Original Codes: 75C, SHST
Type of Depot: TMD
Exam Code: A, Unit
Classes Allocated: 08, 09, 415, 416, 455

Duties Performed: Local shunting, SR (Central) suburban passenger
Notes: A sizeable BR-operated workshop is located at Selhurst, which carried out a number of exams to most of the region's stock

The depot is in the triangle between the Selhurst-Croydon and Norwood Junction-Croydon line, and is visible from the line.

Walking directions: The depot entrance is opposite Selhurst station exit. Walking time less than 5min.

Below:
One of the most important SR depots is Selhurst which has a sizeable EMU servicing depot, shunter depot, repair shop and paint shop. SU has an EMU allocation of over 400 vehicles together with 18 Class 08/09s, which are deployed on all three divisions of the SR. The EMU depot, which has recently been enlarged and modernised, can undertake most repair work. Class 415/4 No 5409 and Class 416/2 No 6277 bask in the sun at SU in May 1985.   *Colin J. Marsden*

Below:
In common with most of the larger depots there are coach washing facilities at Selhurst, although the washing plant is located adjacent to Norwood Junction station. 'Facelifted' 4-EPB No 5415 stands 'in' the washer on 5 May 1982. Selhurst depot is often host to EMUs from other depots which are en route to/from Selhurst repair shop.   *Colin J. Marsden*

Bottom:
Adjacent to the SU running shed is Selhurst repair and paint shop, where a variety of EMU and locomotive repairs, overhauls and modifications can be accomplished. The repair shop is fitted with lifting equipment to enable bogie changes, and most workshop equipment. Class 73 No 73122 rests on accommodation stands in the repair shop on 30 May 1985 while undergoing derailment damage repairs.   *Colin J. Marsden*

TOPS CODE: SW

SWINDON

Location No: 75013
Region: Western
Gazetteer Ref: 9 G 5
Original Codes: 82C
Type of Depot: SD
Exam Code: A

Classes Allocated: 08*
Duties Performed: Local shunting
Notes: Depot also maintains main line traction

There are no actual depot buildings at Swindon depot, and locomotives are fuelled and stabled at the side of the Gloucester line adjacent to the station. The depot is visible from the line.

Walking directions: Entrance to the depot is effected through the official BREL Swindon Works entrance.

* Depot lost its allocation in spring 1987.

Below:
Located between Swindon station and the now closed BREL Works is Swindon depot which had an allocation of just four Class 08s. The depot consists of a small servicing shed spanning one track with a few stabling sidings. In addition to the shunter allocation, SW is often host to main line motive power operating into the area on freight and passenger duties. This general view of the depot taken on 13 April 1980 shows four Class 08s. When the BREL Works were open and carried out shunter overhauls the depot was often host to 'foreign' motive power.
Colin J. Marsden

TOPS CODE: TE

THORNABY

Location No: 15401
Region: Eastern
Gazetteer Ref: 28 E 4
Original Codes: 51L
Type of Depot: TMD
Exam Code: E

Classes Allocated: 08, 20, 31, 37, 47
Duties Performed: Shunting and main line freight
Notes: Wheel lathe. Kingfisher logo. 2×Snowploughs. BTU

The depot is on the east of Thornaby station, to the north of the Middlesbrough line.

Walking directions: Leave Thornaby station by the approach road and turn left into Mandale Road. Fork left into Middlesbrough Road, and the depot entrance is on the left-hand side of this road. Walking time 15min.

Below:
Teesside's main motive power depot at Thornaby is a sizeable complex with service, maintenance and carriage and wagons sections. The depot currently holds an allocation of Classes 08, 20, 31, 37 and 47 locomotives. The main depot consists of an 11-road shed of which five are dedicated to heavy maintenance work. This general view of the east end was taken on 18 May 1982.
Colin J. Marsden

Below:
Four roads of the depot are used for running purposes where locomotives pass
through upon arrival at the depot. If any problems are encountered the locomotive
would be passed to the maintenance factory. This view shows a Class 08 outside
the service depot, while Class 37/0 No 37008 displays a 'Not to be Moved' board in
an adjacent road. Note the 'wait', 'proceed' illuminated boards above the shed
entrances.   Colin J. Marsden

Bottom:
Fuelling facilities are provided at both the east and west ends of the depot and are
of the traditional early 1960s design with roof canopy, as displayed here by the
west end equipment. TE depot undertakes an amount of M&EE work including
locomotive modifications, often entailing other depots' motive power, as well as
some industrial motive power.   Colin J. Marsden

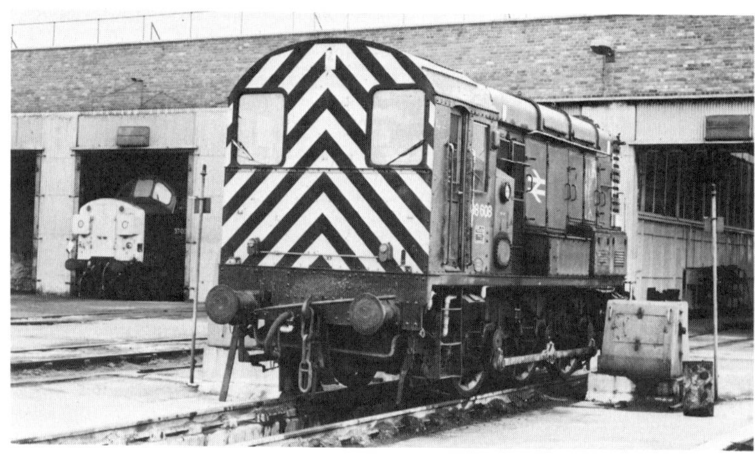

TOPS CODE: TI

TINSLEY

Location No: 25201
Region: Eastern
Gazetteer Ref: 42 G 1
Original Codes: 41A
Type of Depot: TMD
Exam Code: E

Classes Allocated: 08, 20, 31, 37, 45, 47
Duties Performed: Shunting, Yorkshire area freight
Notes: 2×Snowploughs. BTU

The depot is situated on the line from Treeton Junction to Shepcote Lane, and is visible from this line, which does not have any regular passenger services.

Bus directions: Turn right outside Sheffield station and left into Harmer Lane, turn right into Pond Street, leading into Flat Street. Traverse the right side of Fitzalan Square and continue into Haymarket and Waingate. From here board a South Yorkshire PTE No 24 bus bound for Brinsworth, alight at the Three Magpies Hotel in Brinsworth. Bear right at the junction with Brinsworth Road, after passing over the motorway turn right into Wood Lane, and the depot entrance is on the left after crossing the railway bridge. Journey time 45min.

Below:
Another of the large purpose-built modern traction depots is Tinsley (Sheffield). A six-track double-ended building is provided with fuel and service facilities available at either end. TI's 1987 allocation consisted of locomotives of Classes 08, 20, 31, 37, 45 and 47. To the side of the main building a heavy maintenance road is available for lifting and steam cleaning. Class 37/0 No 37194 is seen outside the depot on 27 April 1984. *David Nicholas*

Each of the 12 maintenance roads has wide side platforms, to provide safe access; low level walkways provide wheel and bogie access. TI is fully equipped to service and maintain virtually any type of locomotive, having facilities for power unit and bogie removal. TI is primarily a freight depot, once deploying all its resources around the large Tinsley yard; however, today with the yard being but a shadow of its former self, motive power is spread further afield. *Colin J. Marsden*

TOTON

Location No: 56580
Region: Midland
Gazetteer Ref: 41 G 3
Original Codes: 16A
Type of Depot: TMD
Exam Code: E

Classes Allocated: 08, 20, 56, 58
Duties Performed: Shunting, local and main line passenger and freight traffic
Notes: Wheel lathe. 2×Snowploughs. BTU

The depot is on the west side of the Erewash Valley line between Alfreton and Mansfield Parkway and Trent Junction, and is visible from the line.

Bus directions: From Nottingham: Turn right outside the station into Carrington Street, cross Canel Street and enter the bus station on the right. Here board a Barton No 4A bus, alighting at the now closed Stapleford and Sandiacre station. The depot entrance is just across the bridge. Journey time 45min.

From Derby: Outside the station catch any bus to the city bus station, here change to a Trent No 102 bus bound for Nottingham, and alight at the now closed Stapleford and Sandiacre station, the depot entrance being adjacent to the bridge. Journey time 45min.

Below:
The largest diesel depot in terms of allocation is Toton, near Nottingham, with locomotives of Classes 08, 20, 56 and 58 on its books. The buildings are equally as large with inside accommodation for upwards of 60 locomotives. The main rail approaches to the depot are north facing with large outside storage sidings, the area illustrated here. *Brian Morrison*

Below:
Locomotive fuelling facilities are provided between the main line and depot buildings and can deal with several locomotives simultaneously. Two Class 45s stand by the fuelling equipment in this study.   *Colin J. Marsden*

Bottom:
Areas of the covered accommodation are dedicated to specific operations such as classified overhauls, component replacement and cleaning. This illustration shows the heavy maintenance area, situated on the west side of the complex. The Class 45 No 45110 is seen supported by jacks whilst bogie repairs are carried out, and in the adjoining road BR preserved Class 40 No 40122 (D200) is repaired before its return to traffic in 1983.   *John Tuffs*

TYSELEY

Location No: 66425
Region: Midland
Gazetteer Ref: 15 G 5
Original Codes: 2A
Type of Depot: TMD
Exam Code: E, Unit

Duties Performed: Shunting, West Midlands local passenger
Notes: Depot also maintains main line traction. Wheel lathe

Classes Allocated: 08, 101, 108, 115, 116, 118, 119, 121, 122, 127, 128

The depot is on the west side of the line north of the station and is visible from the line.

Walking directions: Turn right outside the station, and right at the end of the bridge into Warwick Road, and the depot entrance is on the right-hand side. Walking time 5min.

Bus directions: From Birmingham New Street: Depart from New Street station and follow the signs to Stephenson Street. Turn right into Stephenson Place, right again into New Street, and left into High Street. From here board a West Midlands PTE No 44 bus bound for Lincoln Road, and alight at the depot entrance. Journey time 30min.

Below:
The Birmingham area DMU fleet is maintained by Tyseley depot which also has an allocation of Class 08s for local pilot operation. In addition to its DMU operation TS also has service and repair facilities for main line traction, taking in repair work from other LM depots. A Class 120/101/120 formation is seen at the depot on 23 June 1984 led by car No 53694. *Michael J. Collins*

TOPS CODE: VR

VALE OF RHEIDOL

Location No: None
Region: Midland
Gazetteer Ref: 13 C 5
Original Codes: 6F
Type of Depot: Steam

Exam Code: Special
Classes Allocated: 98, CS
Duties Performed: Vale of Rheidol narrow gauge services

The depot is between the standard and narrow gauge systems, at the east of the station, and is visible from the line.

Walking directions: Depot access is via a footpath from the station platform. Walking time less than 5min.

Below:
BR's sole surviving steam line, The Vale of Rheidol, which has three locomotives, has its depot facilities at Aberystwyth where a small shed/works is located. All stock is usually maintained and repaired here with locomotives visiting a BREL works (formerly Swindon) for classified attention. Vale of Rheidol No 9 *Prince of Wales* stands outside the shed taking water in June 1969.   *John Tuffs*

TOPS CODE: WC

WATERLOO & CITY

Location No: 87211
Region: Southern
Gazetteer Ref: 40 D 5
Original Codes: None
Type of Depot: EMUD

Exam Code: Unit
Classes Allocated: 487
Duties Performed: Waterloo & City line

The depot is situated at the Waterloo end of the Waterloo & City line, east of the station, and is visible from the platforms.

Walking directions: Access to the depot is by a narrow footpath from the east end of the Bank-bound platform. **WARNING: This path is adjacent to live rails, and staff permission must be obtained before proceeding past the platform end.** Walking time less than 5min.

Below:
The isolated Waterloo & City underground line owned by BR, has full workshop and stabling facilities at the Waterloo end of the line. There are seven sidings, two of which have shed accommodation, where all classified attention is carried out. A Driving and Trailer vehicle are seen stabled in 1982. *Colin J. Marsden*

TOPS CODE: WD

WIMBLEDON

Location No: 87252
Region: Southern
Gazetteer Ref: 39 F 5
Original Codes: WM, WDON
Type of Depot: EMUD
Exam Code: Unit

Classes Allocated: 414, 423, 455
Duties Performed: SR/Western section local/main line passenger
Notes: Wheel lathe. BTU

The depot is on the west side of the line north of the station and is visible from the line.

Walking directions: Turn right outside Wimbledon station into Wimbledon Hill, turn right again into Alexandra Road and continue into Strathearn Road, and Home Park Road. Turn right into Arthur Road past Wimbledon Park LRT station, and at the bottom turn right into Durnsford Road, and the depot entrance is on the left just prior to the railway bridge. Walking time from Wimbledon 20min and Wimbledon Park 5min.

Below:
The Southern's Western Section principal EMU depot is Wimbledon, which is a large complex consisting of 23 stabling sidings at Wimbledon Park, and 17 stabling sidings and seven shed roads at East Wimbledon. In 1986 the depot had an allocation of 167 EMU sets made up of 618 coaches. Wimbledon East is a comparatively new depot, replacing the former Durnsford Road depot in the early 1970s. Nos 9-11 shed roads of the 'new depot' are illustrated, accommodating two Class 508 and one 4-VEP unit.   *Colin J. Marsden*

Below:
All routine maintenance requirements for SR EMU stock can be carried out at East Wimbledon. Of the seven shed roads, five are dedicated to routine maintenance such as brake block changing and technical examination, while two are deemed as lifting roads, used for heavy maintenance, having an overhead gantry crane. Two Class 455s Nos 5836 and 5857 stand in the servicing area in early 1986.
Colin J. Marsden

Bottom:
In late 1985 a Wheel Lathe shop was commissioned at East Wimbledon, which is now responsible for all SR-allocated EMUs and locomotives. The Lathe Shop is a single track shed being approximately two coach lengths long and double ended. Class 455 No 5843 is seen in the Lathe Shop on 31 January 1986.
Colin J. Marsden

TOPS CODE: WN

WILLESDEN

Location No: 72271
Region: Midland
Gazetteer Ref: 39 C 4
Original Codes: 1A
Type of Depot: TMD
Exam Code: B, J

Classes Allocated: 08, 82, 83, 86, 87
Duties Performed: WCML passenger and freight, local shunting
Notes: Wheel lathe. BTU

The depot is situated between the ac and dc electric lines at the south end of the station (low-level platforms), and is visible from both running lines and the high-level station.

Walking directions: Turn left outside the barrier at Willesden low-level platforms into a drive which leads under the high level lines and into the depot. Walking time 5min.

Below:
The London Midland Region-London AC depot is located at Willesden, where a 6-road shed is to be found. As well as dealing with electric traction WN has facilities for diesels, with fuelling apparatus at the London end. The shed is divided into two 3-road sections, one dealing with heavy repairs and classified maintenance, and the other stabling and service checks. Class 87 No 87006 receives its short-lived dark grey paint scheme in one of the maintenance roads on 11 May 1984, while technicians install the Brecknell-Willis high speed pantograph. *Colin J. Marsden*

Below:
WN is responsible for the entire Class 82, 83, 86 and 87 fleets, giving a total of over
140 locomotives. To facilitate bogie removal and thus traction motor attention,
synchronised Matterson screw jacks are provided, seen here in use on Class 86/2
No 86223 in May 1984. The lifting of locomotives at WN is usually carried out in
No 6 yard.   *Colin J. Marsden*

Bottom:
In No 3 road there is a wheel reprofiling lathe, used not only by the WN allocation
but also by BY-allocated EMUs, as demonstrated in this picture of Class 310
No 310077 positioned over the equipment. Adjacent to the shed on both the main
line and DC line sides, there are a number of stabling sidings in which, amongst
other things, the depot crane and overhead line maintenance train are stabled.
Colin J. Marsden

YORK

Location No: 16412
Region: Eastern
Gazetteer Ref: 21 C 5
Original Codes: 50A, 55B
Type of Depot: SD
Exam Code: A

Classes Allocated: 08
Duties Performed: Local shunting
Notes: Depot also maintains main line traction.
3×Snowploughs

The depot is north of the station, both sides of the main line, and is visible from the line.

Walking directions: Turn left outside the station into Station Road, and turn left again into Leeman Road. The depot entrance is on the right-hand side, just after the Railway Museum. Walking time 10min.

York's locomotive allocation is now maintained in the work's area.

Below:
Until the early 1980s York had a sizeable diesel depot with a main line allocation sited adjacent to the National Railway Museum complex. However, this building has now been taken over as part of the Museum and locomotive inspection facilities moved slightly northwards. York Class 03 No 03089 together with its match truck, stand next to the fuel and water supplies. *Colin J. Marsden*

RAILWAY TECHNICAL CENTRE DERBY

Location No: 57421
Jurisdiction: BRB
Original Codes: None
Type of Depot: Research Centre
Exam Code: Special
Classes Allocated: 97 various departmental unit stock

Duties Performed: Research and test duties
Notes: HQ — Railway Technical Centre also undertakes test operations on traffic locomotives and stock

The Railway Technical Centre is on the west side of the main Trent-Derby line, south of Derby station, and is visible from the line.

Walking directions: Go straight ahead outside Derby station into Midland Road, and left at the traffic lights into London Road. Cross the railway bridge, and the main gate to the Railway Technical Centre is on the left. Walking time 15min.
NOTE: There is strictly no admittance to this location.

Below:
Although not a running and maintenance depot, the Railway Technical Centre at Derby does have a locomotive, DMU and coaching stock allocation. Most modifications, alterations and repairs are effected in the complex, but fuelling and servicing is more usually carried out in the Etches Park Diesel Depot on the opposite side of the MR main line. Red and blue liveried No 97201 and some test vehicles are seen outside the vehicle laboratory   *Colin J. Marsden*

BREL and BRML

Visits can usually be arranged to BREL establishments with prior permission of the relevant Works Manager. Again it must be emphasised that **casual visits are completely out of the question, and persons caught on company property will be dealt with severely**. Initial applications should be addressed thus. At most works a ban on photography exists.

BREL Crewe

BREL House, West Street, Crewe CW1 3JB.

BREL Derby Litchurch Lane

Carriage & Wagon Works, Litchurch Lane, Derby DE2 8AD.

BREL Derby Locomotive

Locomotive Works, Station Approach, Derby DE1 2RZ.

BREL York

Carriage Works, Holgate Road, York YO2 4DJ.

The following BREL establishments were handed over to **British Rail Maintenance Ltd** on 31 March 1987, as a subsidiary of the BRB.

BRML Doncaster

PO Box 29, Doncaster, South Yorkshire DN1 1PD.

BRML Eastleigh

Campbell Road, Eastleigh, Southampton, Hampshire SO5 5ZB.

BRML Glasgow

Locomotive Works, Station Approach, Derby DE1 2RZ.

BRML Glasgow

BRML, Charles Street, Glasgow.

BRML Wolverton

Carriage Works, Stratford Road, Wolverton, Milton Keynes MK12 5NT.

The responsibility for major overhauls to Classes 37, 47, 56, 81, 85, 86 and 87 falls on BREL Crewe, which is the largest of the BREL workshops, with often upwards of 60 locomotives present at one time. New building projects at Crewe Works presently include the Class 90 electric locomotives, and Class 91 Electra locomotives for ECML use. Class 47/4 No 47453 stands in the works Paint Shop receiving body attention prior to final painting. *Colin J. Marsden*

SAFE WORKING
LOAD 15 TONS

BREL Derby Litchurch Lane Works is responsible for coaching stock construction, railbus assembly, IC125 trailer stock repairs, coaching stock repairs and wagon overhauls. In addition to operations for BR the works carries out contracts for overseas and private customers. Two BR Mk 3 sleeper vehicles are seen under construction in this April 1982 illustration.   *Colin J. Marsden*

Bottom:
Located opposite Derby station, BREL's Derby Locomotive Works is responsible for IC125 power car overhauls, Class 45 classified attention (now being run down), and Class 08 and 20 overhauls. Other works operations include wheel manufacture and repair, power unit overhauls, and ancillary equipment repairs. Class 45/0 No 45012 is seen undergoing front end repairs in this September 1985 view.   *Colin J. Marsden*

Below:
The former BREL Doncaster Works is now one of the BR Maintenance Ltd locations and is responsible for Class 31, 37, 50 and 58 overhauls, as well as some coaching stock and wagon repairs. In recent years the main 'new build' operation has been the construction of Classes 56 and 58, but in the future new build projects are likely to be carried out at other works. Class 58 No 58036 stands outside the works Weigh Shop on 4 February 1986 prior to commissioning.   *Colin J. Marsden*

Below:
The most southerly of the BRML establishments is Eastleigh where SR
locomotives and EMU repairs are effected. Some ER EMUs and various
locomotive-hauled vehicles are also given attention at the works. A Class 415
DMBS and various Class 423 coaches are seen being prepared for painting in the
Paint Shop, on 18 September 1985. Usually around six locomotives and 45 EMUs
vehicles are receiving attention at one time. *Colin J. Marsden*

Bottom:
The sizeable works complex at Glasgow, the former BREL works, is responsible for
ScR-allocated Class 08, 20 and 26 locomotive overhauls, together with EMU
and coaching stock attention. In this 1980 view of the main locomotive area
various Classes 26 and 27 can be seen. *Tom Noble*

Below:
No locomotive activity is undertaken at Wolverton, the main brief being the overhaul of coaching stock vehicles, including many EMU types. Another function of the works is the storage of the Royal Train vehicles when not in use. This illustration shows a Mk 2f FO No 3289 on one of the traversers. *BR*

Bottom:
The major unit stock production works is BREL York, where most new generation EMU and DMU sets have been constructed. In addition to new build operations, a sizeable part of the works is dedicated to coaching stock repairs. In this general view of the New Build Shop, various Class 317, 318 and 150 cars can be seen taking shape. *Colin J. Marsden*

Below:
In August 1987 the Class 87/2 was reclassified as Class 90 prior to the first locomotive taking to the road. In this illustration No 87201 now 90001 is seen inside BREL Crewe Works in advanced stages of construction during July 1987.   *Colin J. Marsden*